The Concept of Definiteness and Its Application to Automated Reference Resolution

BERKELEY
INSIGHTS
IN LINGUISTICS
AND SEMIOTICS

Irmengard Rauch
General Editor

Vol. 69

PETER LANG
New York • Washington, D.C./Baltimore • Bern
Frankfurt am Main • Berlin • Brussels • Vienna • Oxford

Zaur Kambarov

The Concept of Definiteness and Its Application to Automated Reference Resolution

English and German

PETER LANG
New York • Washington, D.C./Baltimore • Bern
Frankfurt am Main • Berlin • Brussels • Vienna • Oxford

Library of Congress Cataloging-in-Publication Data

Kambarov, Zaur.
The concept of definiteness and its application to automated reference
resolution: English and German / Zaur Kambarov.
p. cm. — (Berkeley insights in linguistics and semiotics; vol. 69)
Includes bibliographical references.
1. Definiteness (Linguistics). 2. Grammar, Comparative and general—
Determiners. 3. Computational linguistics.
4. Reference (Linguistics). I. Title.
P299.D43K36 415—dc22 2008003455
ISBN 978-1-4331-0224-0
ISSN 0893-6935

Bibliographic information published by **Die Deutsche Bibliothek**.
Die Deutsche Bibliothek lists this publication in the "Deutsche
Nationalbibliografie"; detailed bibliographic data is available
on the Internet at http://dnb.ddb.de/.

Contents

Acknowledgments ... vii
List of Symbols and Abbreviations ... ix

1. Introduction ... 1
   1.1 The Problem of Applying the Concept of Definiteness to Reference Resolution ... 1
   1.2 Definiteness as a Matter of Degree ... 2
   1.3 Approach and Objectives ... 4
   1.4 Overview of the Present Study ... 4

2. The Current State of Research on Definiteness and Nominal Reference Resolution ... 7
   2.1 Defining Definiteness ... 7
   2.2 Semantic Subcategorization of Nouns ... 10
   2.3 Representation of Determiners in an X-bar and in a Construction Grammar ... 12
   2.4 Nominal Reference Resolution ... 15

3. On the Concept of Definiteness ... 19
   3.1 Selected Ontology ... 19
   3.2 A Set of Rules for the Use of the Articles ... 20
   3.3 Analysis of Data from Modern German and English ... 25
   3.4 Evaluation of Results ... 44

4. Application of the Concept of Definiteness in a Reference Resolution Algorithm ... 47
   4.1 A Unification Parser ... 47
   4.2 A Heuristic for Ordering Known Spaces ... 55
   4.3 The Algorithm for Nominal Reference Resolution ... 55
   4.4 Analysis of Data from Modern English and Evaluation of Results ... 58

5. Application of the Proposed Approach to Data from Earlier Periods of the German Language 73
5.1 Old High German 73
5.2 Middle High German 86
5.3 Early New High German 104
5.4 Evaluation of Results 124

6. Conclusion 127

Appendix A. Implementation of the Algorithm for Nominal Reference Resolution 129

Appendix B. Implementation of the Heuristic for Ordering Known Spaces 135

Bibliography 141

Acknowledgments

I would like to thank my research advisor Professor Irmengard Rauch for her invaluable help and guidance, Professor Werner Abraham for supporting my application to the graduate program at UC Berkeley, and Professor Jerome Feldman for his suggestions on computational aspects of this work.

Symbols and Abbreviations

$\wedge$	and
$\vee$	or
$\Rightarrow$	implies
$\forall$	for all
$\exists$	exists
$\in$	belongs to
cat	category
DEF-ART	definite article
Det	determiner
Eg.	English
fem.	feminine
Gk.	Greek
I	Inflectional Phrase
INDEF-ART	indefinite article
instr.	instrumental
LF	List of Features
masc.	masculine
MR	mental representation
MS	mental space
N	noun
neut.	neuter
Nnon_max	non-maximal projection of a Noun Phrase
NP	Noun Phrase, a maximal projection
RE	referring expression
pl.	plural
PL	plural (in computer print-outs)
REF	reference
Q	quantifier
quantif	quantifier

r	rule (in text annotations); repeat (with sentence numbers)
s	mental space (in text annotations)
sem	semantic
sg.	singular
SG	singular (in computer print-outs)
Vnon_max	non-maximal projection of a Verb Phrase
VP	Verb Phrase, a maximal projection
ZERO-ART	zero article

Symbols and Abbreviations

$\wedge$	and
$\vee$	or
$\Rightarrow$	implies
$\forall$	for all
$\exists$	exists
$\in$	belongs to
cat	category
DEF-ART	definite article
Det	determiner
Eg.	English
fem.	feminine
Gk.	Greek
I	Inflectional Phrase
INDEF-ART	indefinite article
instr.	instrumental
LF	List of Features
masc.	masculine
MR	mental representation
MS	mental space
N	noun
neut.	neuter
Nnon_max	non-maximal projection of a Noun Phrase
NP	Noun Phrase, a maximal projection
RE	referring expression
pl.	plural
PL	plural (in computer print-outs)
REF	reference
Q	quantifier
quantif	quantifier

r	rule (in text annotations); repeat (with sentence numbers)
s	mental space (in text annotations)
sem	semantic
sg.	singular
SG	singular (in computer print-outs)
Vnon_max	non-maximal projection of a Verb Phrase
VP	Verb Phrase, a maximal projection
ZERO-ART	zero article

• CHAPTER ONE •

Introduction

1.1 The Problem of Applying the Concept of Definiteness to Reference Resolution

A typical grammatical reference work addressing the concept of definiteness usually contains a large number of rules with numerous exceptions and special cases (e.g. H.-J. Grimm 1987: Chap. 1–3, DUDEN 1998:213–221, Flämig 1991:473–478), which hinders effective use of information provided by determiners in nominal reference resolution. There exists a need for a description of the category of definiteness that would be concise and free of contradictions, so that it can be used in a reference resolution algorithm. Yet such a description should contain enough detail in order to fully explain and utilize determiners in a text. Popescu-Belis (2003:297) in a recent paper on reference resolution (cf. Chap. 2 below) remarks on the effect of using an oversimplified view of determiners in his analysis: "…these scores confirm that the links between definiteness and reference are subtler than the present rules."

The central problem in reference resolution is distinguishing between instances of coreference and cases when nominal phrases are used to introduce new entities into an ongoing discourse. Karttunen (1976:365) was the first to suggest that a reference resolution system should process Referring Expressions (REs) using representations— *object files*—of entities of the real world. Appelt and Kronfeld (1987:643) proposed to use a set of features for each entity. Updates to such sets are made according to referring acts, defined on the basis of the speech act theory. Lappin and Leass (1994:535) suggested ordering discourse referents according to their contextual *salience*. When a noun phrase referring to a new entity is processed, a representation for it is added to the discourse model. For each such representation a salience value is computed. This value is updated after processing every new sentence. The referent of a pronoun is the entity with the highest salience at that moment. Although salience depends on syntactic characteristics of referring expressions, the most important factor for (re)computing it is simply sentence recency. If an entity is not mentioned in the current sentence, its value as a potential referent decreases by half.

Byron and Allen (2002:80) discuss an interface for implementations of a reference resolution component for dialog systems. The interface is based on a model that defines reference resolution as a mapping from initial RE descriptions to final logical term descriptions, which include a referent when one can be found. A referent is viewed as an extension—an object from the domain of interpretation (Allen et al. 1996:65). For example, the referent of the expression *President Putin* would be a token from the system's database, e.g. VLADIMIR-PUTIN. Among attributes considered to be important for building a semantic representation of an RE Byron and Allen (2002:82) indicate both Specificity—Definite or Indefinite—and Givenness—grammatically marked accessibility as presented in Gundel et al. (1993:275).

1.2 Definiteness as a Matter of Degree

Current research on definiteness has been significantly influenced by the paper *Cognitive status and the form of referring expressions in discourse* (Gundel et al. 1993). The authors suggest that determiners and some pronouns enable the addressee of a sentence to restrict the set of possible referents of a noun. The use of determiners and pronominal forms depends on the degree of definiteness of a referent. The following givenness hierarchy is proposed:

in focus	>	activated	>	familiar	>	uniquely identifiable	>	referential	>	type identifiable
{*it*}		{*that*, *this*, *this* N}		{ *that* N}		{*the* N}		{indefinite *this* N}		{*a* N}

Figure 1.1: A givenness hierarchy proposed by Gundel et al. (1993:275).

A particular form can be used only if the corresponding cognitive status is met. The statuses in the scheme above are implicationally related, e.g. an entity that is uniquely identifiable must also be referential, and type identifiable.

The least amount of knowledge on the side of the hearer is presupposed by the use of the indefinite article. "Type identifiable" means that the hearer is expected to know only the properties of the category corresponding to the noun:

(1.1) I couldn't sleep last night. A dog (next door) kept me awake.

To understand an expression with referential (colloquial) *this* N the addressee must either retrieve an existing representation of the referent or construct a new one. The referent is always a particular object:

(1.2) I couldn't sleep last night. This dog (next door) kept me awake.

The speaker can use the definite article only if the hearer can identify the referent on the basis of the nominal alone. Gundel et al. (1993:278) write:

> FAMILIAR: The addressee is able to uniquely identify the intended referent because he already has a representation of it in memory (in long-term memory if it has not been recently mentioned or perceived, or in short-term memory if it has). This status is... sufficient for appropriate use of the demonstrative determiner *that*.

Thus nouns whose referents are uniquely identifiable but not familiar can be used with *the* but not with *that*. It seems that the only candidates here are elements of frames that have not been previously mentioned in the ongoing discourse.

The status of a referent is "activated" if it is represented in current short-term memory. It may have been retrieved from long-term memory or be present in the immediate linguistic or extralinguistic context. This status is sufficient for the demonstrative pronoun *that* and for stressed personal pronouns. *That* in

(1.3) I couldn't sleep last night. That kept me awake.

makes sense if a barking dog was just mentioned or if the addressee can actually hear it. In such cases *this* can also be used but it requires that the referent be not only activated, but speaker-activated.

In-focus means that the referent is at the current center of attention. The entities in focus are that subset of activated entities which are likely to be continued as topics of subsequent utterances.

1.3 Approach and Objectives

We adopt the view of reference that has become common in linguistics (Sidner 1981:218, Popescu-Belis 2003:290). Referents of nouns in a text are considered to be elements of one of several alternating *mental spaces*, which form a level of conceptual organization between the text and reality (Fauconnier 1985:15, Langacker 2001:184). Truth values can be assigned to entities and relations between entities in a mental space based on what is known about the corresponding real situation at the time of discourse, as well as common knowledge organized in hierarchical structures—frames. A mental space is often an instantiated frame (Fauconnier 1985:91). It is generally agreed that knowledge of frames plays an important role in choosing which determiner to use with a given noun. Thus determiners can be interpreted as signals helping the receiver to manipulate mental constructs containing referents of nouns.

In this work we present a set of uniform rules that appear to capture the factors essential to the concept of definiteness. We show how a carefully chosen ontology can help adequately describe the use of articles. It turns out that the same principles govern the choice of the definite, indefinite and zero articles before count nouns, mass nouns, plurals and even abstract nouns. We are discussing primarily the English and German article systems, but most of our discussion is also applicable to other languages that have articles. In addition to data from Modern English and German, we also analyze fragments from all major periods of the history of the German language.

We demonstrate that using concepts related to the category of definiteness and taking into account information expressed by determiners in a text can help create realistic and robust reference representations. We propose an algorithm for nominal reference resolution that uses the definiteness value of each determiner phrase to guide the search for its referent. It organizes referents of all encountered nouns in structures that correspond to mental spaces that are being described. Our system includes a unification parser that uses a special set of syntactic and semantic features to extract information relevant for identifying referents.

1.4 Overview of the Present Study

Chapter 1 introduces the problems associated with the concept of definiteness and its applicability in Natural Language Processing. Chapter 2 presents both semantic and syntactic aspects of the current research on definiteness, as well as modern approaches to automated reference resolution.

In Chapter 3 we discuss an ontology suitable for a description of determiners and formulate a set of eight uniform rules for the use of the definite, indefinite and zero articles in English and German. Further, we evaluate applicability of the formulated rules to example sentences and text fragments from English and German prose.

Chapter 4 presents an algorithm for nominal reference resolution. We also describe and evaluate the performance of an automated reference resolution system based on an implementation of the reference resolution algorithm.

Chapter 5 demonstrates application of the proposed approach to text fragments from all three major historical variants of the German language.

CHAPTER TWO

The Current State of Research on Definiteness and Nominal Reference Resolution

2.1 Defining Definiteness

The term *article* originates from Gk. *ἄρθρον* (*arthron* 'joint'). Aristotle was the first to use this term in the context of a discussion of literary texts in his *Poetics*, composed around 350 B.C. According to Aristotle, all words can be divided into categories based on a combination of their meaning, form and function. These categories were used to capture the organization of *λεξις* (*lexis*), which for the author of *Poetics* was material available to a creator of a literary text. *Lexis* could be translated as 'verbal expression' (of thought), yet often less accurate terms are used, for example, 'language' in the excerpt below—and Aristotle's *μέρη λέξεως* have simply become 'parts of speech'. Here is the famous fragment from Part XX of *Poetics*, translated by S.H. Butcher (1898:70–75):

Της δε λεξεως απασης ταδ' εστι τα μερη, στοιχειον, συλλαβη, συνδεσμος, ονομα, ρημα, αρθρον, πτωσις, λογος... αρθρον δ' εστι φωνη ασημος η λογου αρχην η τελος η διορισμον δυλοι, οιον το φυμι και το περι και τα αλλα.	Language in general includes the following parts: Letter, Syllable, Connecting word, Noun, Verb, Inflection or Case, Sentence or Phrase... A Connecting word is a non-significant sound, which marks the beginning, end, or division of a sentence.

The Stoics distinguished four parts of speech: noun, verb, syndesmos, and arthron. Arthron was an element of a sentence with case endings, which expressed the gender and number of nouns, such as *ho, he, to* and *hoi, hai, ta* (Gk. masc., fem. and neut. articles, sing. and pl.). Arthrons included what we would call today pronouns and articles. Personal and demonstrative pronouns were 'definite' (ἄρθρα ὡρισμένα), and articles and relative pronouns were 'indefinite' arthrons (ἄρθρα ἀοριστώδη) (Krámský 1972:18).

The eight parts of speech of Dionysius Thrax (born about 166 B.C.) and Apollonius Dyscolus (2nd cent. A.D.) included noun, verb, participle, article (*ἄρθρον*), pronoun (*ἀνεωνυμια*), preposition, adverb and conjunction (Dinneen 1967:93). This system was applied to Latin by Remnius Palaemon (1st cent. A.D.), who replaced article as a part of speech by interjection. In imitation of Greek, some Latin grammarians called their pronouns *hic, haec,* and *hoc* articles. Donatus distinguished the dependent use of *hic* as an article from its use as a demonstrative pronoun. Just like the arthron of the Stoics, Varro's (116–27 B.C.) *pronomen articulare* could be either *finite* (the pronoun) or *infinite* (the article). The Latin demonstrative pronoun *hic* was considered an *articulus finitus*, therefore later German *der*, English *the*, and French *le* were also called definite articles.

One of the first linguistic papers dedicated to the articles was published in the late 19th century by Grasserie (1896). In that paper the principal function of an article was described as individualization of a given subject (Grasserie 1896:286). Guillaume (1919) expressed the view that a noun can have a potential and an effectual meaning. A noun in language has only the ability (*puissance*) to represent objects, while a noun in speech actually represents one or several objects. Some languages developed a system of relationships between potential and real nouns. The article is the visible expression of such relationships (Guillaume 1919:21–22). Representing a particular object and an abstract class are two extremes, between which intermediate states (or types of referring: *étendues*) can exist. This idea is similar to the view prevalent in recent research on determiners, according to which each use of a noun in a discourse can be characterized by one of several possible degrees of definiteness (Gundel et al. 1993).

Christophersen (1939:30) suggests dividing all nouns into *unit-words* and *continuate-words*. A unit-word represents a single object—a member of a class of similar objects, which is "viewed as a point". Christophersen's continuate-words appear to be a generalization of the concept of a mass noun: he describes them as referring to something extended indefinitely in space or time. A particular shape is only possible if an "outer mold" is present. Examples of unit-words include *girl, house, day, system, event*; examples of continuate-words are *butter, water, iron, music, hunger, leisure*.

The definite article used with a unit-word shows that some association with previously acquired knowledge has been added to the potential meaning of a word. Such knowledge is not part of the concept corresponding to the noun, therefore this case is similar to the use of a proper noun. A noun with an indefinite article does not refer to a particular object known to the speaker and the hearer. No knowledge other than the "idea of the word itself" is involved and the object appears to be chosen at random from its whole class (Christophersen 1939:32). This view is quite common, both in linguistics and in logic. Frege claimed that language expresses the distinction between *Gegenstand* and *Begriff* ('object' and 'concept') using the definite and the indefinite articles, respectively (Frege 1892:194). Behaghel in his *Deutsche Syntax* (1923:45) wrote: "Der unbestimmte Artikel hat die Aufgabe, aus verschiedenen Vertretern einer Gattung einen einzelnen herauszuheben."

According to Christophersen (1939:33), the zero article is used with continuate-words when they refer to:

1. the whole genus everywhere and at all times (toto-generic sense):

(2.1) Lead is heavier than iron.

(2.2) Time is money.

(2.3) History repeats itself.

2. an indefinite amount of the genus (parti-generic sense):

(2.4) We are going to have tea soon.

(2.5) You are drawing water with a sieve.

(2.6) There is still frost in the ground.

(2.7) I have caused sorrow already.

3. in negations (nulli-generic sense):

(2.8) I have not tasted food for three days.

(2.9) They never get rain in summer.

Vater (1979:115) stated that the "system of German articles" includes *jeder, dieser, jener,* possessive pronouns, *aller, der,* zero, *ein, mehrere, einige(r), irgendwelche(r), irgendein, mancher.* The morpheme *d-* of the definite article has only a "general, abstract" meaning, and thus always requires knowledge of the context. The function of the definite article is to separate a class from other classes:

(2.10) *Der Baum ist eine Pflanze.*
DEF-ART tree is INDEF-ART plant.

or one or several particular representatives of a class from all its other members:

(2.11) *Der Baum im Garten blüht.*
DEF-ART tree in DEF-ART garden is blossoming.

(2.12) *Die Bäume im Garten blühen.*
DEF-ART trees in DEF-ART garden are blossoming.

2.2 Semantic Subcategorization of Nouns

Löbner (1985:292) proposes to distinguish between sortal and relational nouns:

> Sortal nouns classify objects, whereas relational nouns describe objects as standing in a certain relation to others. These are two fundamentally different ways to characterize objects, and one cannot be reduced to the other.

As an example, the concepts *woman* and *wife* are compared. The first is a sortal noun. Logically, it is a one-place predicate—a conjunction of other one-place predicates such as *human, female, adult.* The referent of a relational noun, on the other hand, can only be determined based on a relationship between two or more objects. A woman can be referred to as a *wife* only if the relationship *being married* holds between her and a man. An important subclass of relational nouns are functional nouns. Their reference is defined by one-to-one logical functions. Functional concepts can refer only to one object. For instance, *weight* is a function whose domain are physical objects and whose range are values on a certain scale. An object can have only one weight, which can be referred to as *the weight* of that object. A relational noun does not belong to the class of functional nouns if its definition involves a relation that is not a function (e.g. one-to-many). Such concepts include, e.g.

kinship terms: *sister, daugter, aunt, cousin, grandmother;*

social relations: *neighbour, room-mate.*

Löbner states that the definitions above "apply to uses or occurrences of nouns rather than to nouns as such" (1985:292).

Definte NPs are divided into "semantic definites" and "pragmatic definites". The referents of the former are established independently of the immediate situation or context of the utterance, while the latter are unambiguous only if the corresponding situation or context are known. Semantic definites always represent functional concepts. This explains the use of the definite article in cases where the overall reference of an NP is not determined (Löbner 1985:302):

(2.13) the mayor of a small town in Wales

(2.14) the mother of one of my students

In these examples we cannot use a noun with the definite article to refer to the object corresponding to *small town* or *one of my students*, but we can use definite NPs to refer to the mayor of that town or the mother of that student. The function expressed by the concepts mayor and mother establishes a one-to-one link between indefinite and definite referents.

In sentences like

(2.15) He was taken to (the) hospital.

(2.16) She goes to church.

(2.17) He came after lunch.

the nouns do not "refer to any particular object but rather to an abstract situation, in which a hospital, a school, a lunch is an essential constituent" (Löbner 1985:280). In such cases the article is often omitted in English, but not in German:

(2.18) Sie geht in die Kirche.
She goes to DEF-ART church.

(2.19) Er kam nach dem Mittagessen.
He comes after DEF-ART lunch.

Löbner claims that the meaning of the definite article is essentially the same in different languages. Possible variations are due to the fact that the meaning of an NP constrains the use of the articles but does not determine it. For instance, in English a possessive pronoun is often used in cases where in German the definite article is preferred (Löbner 1985:307):

(2.20) English: *He kept his hand in his pocket.*

(2.21) German: *Er hatte die Hand in der Tasche.*

2.3 Representation of Determiners in an X-bar and in a Construction Grammar

In an X-bar grammar (Jackendoff 1977:105) a noun may require a determiner or a Determiner Phrase in order to form a maximal projection. The general pattern is

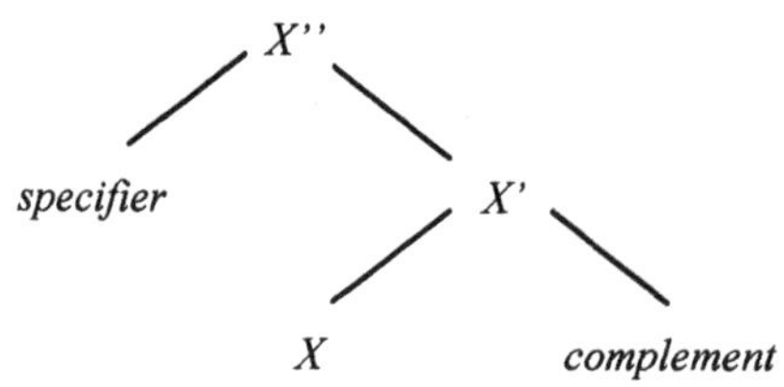

where *X* is the head of the phrase with projections *X'* and *X''*.

The phrase *the student* can be represented as

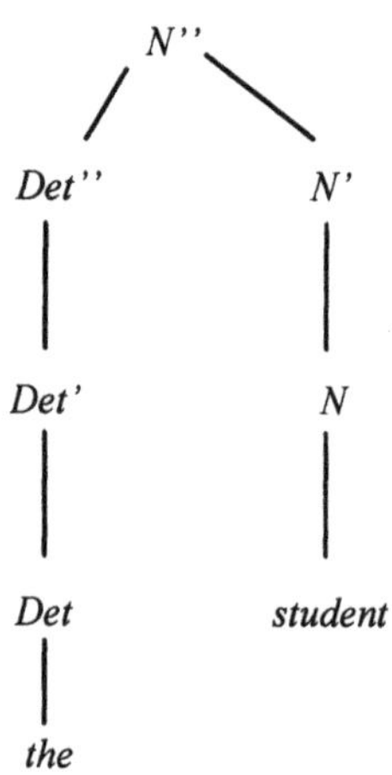

The noun *student* by itself can only form the projection *N'*, therefore if the rule for a whole sentence is

$$I'' \rightarrow N'' I'$$

where I'' stands for Inflectional Phrase, and there is no rule

$$N'' \rightarrow N'$$

or

$$N'' \rightarrow \textit{student}$$

we will not be able to find a parse for a sentence beginning with *student* followed by a verb (without a preceding article).

Fillmore (1988:35) proposes to use complex sets of features, instead of simple atomic categories, to label the units of structure of a sentence. This allows direct representation of the required properties of subordinate constituents. Fillmore calls his approach a Construction Grammar. A construction is defined as follows (Fillmore 1988:36):

> By grammatical construction we mean any syntactic pattern which is assigned one or more conventional functions in a language, together with whatever is linguistically conventionalized about its contribution to the meaning or the use of structures containing it.

On the level of syntax, each construction has internal and external properties. The former characterize the structure and composition of a construction, while the latter describe a construction as a whole, e.g. its function in a larger syntactic context.

Fillmore uses a boxes-within-boxes notation in which information about the external requirements of a construction is placed in the perimeter of the box, with smaller boxes drawn inside to display the construction's internal syntax. This notation is convenient for representing complex sets of attributes. Each attribute is a name-value pair in parentheses.

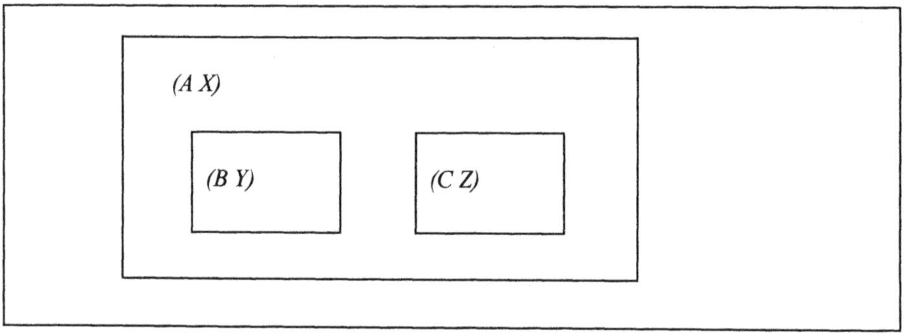

Figure 2.1: Representing sets of attributes using the boxes-within-boxes notation .

In Figure 2.1, a category with the value *X* of the attribute *A* requires two constituents. The value of the attribute *B* of the first constituent must be equal to *Y*, and the value of the attribute *C* of the second constituent must be *Z*.

The basic phrasal categories are represented by the attribute *category*, abbreviated *cat*, e.g. *(cat N), (cat V)*. The levels of headed constructions are characterized in terms of maximal and minimal categories. Maximal categories fill major structural positions in constructions. For instance, a maximal NP will be represented as

(cat N) (max +)

The English determination construction can be represented in the following way:

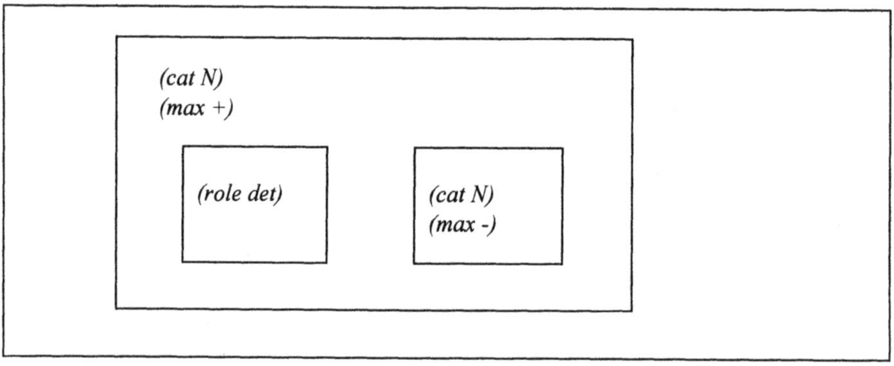

Figure 2.2: A representation of the English determination construction (Fillmore 1988:40).

Articles, as well as possessive and demonstrative pronouns, will be marked in the lexicon as possessing the determiner role (*role det*). For the second slot maximality value '–' is required, e.g. we would not be able to fill it with a pronoun or a proper noun. For proper nouns, mass nouns and count nouns the maximality values are set as follows (Fillmore 1988:40):

proper noun:	*(cat N) (max +)*
mass noun:	*(cat N) (max <unspecified>)*
singular count noun:	*(cat N) (max -)*

2.4 Nominal Reference Resolution

Recent research on Nominal Reference Resolution most closely related to our topic is, in our opinion, best represented by Byron and Allen (2002) and Popescu-Belis (2003).

The first paper discusses an interface for implementations of a reference resolution component for dialog systems. Reference resolution is defined as a mapping from initial RE descriptions to final logical term descriptions. A referent is an object from the domain of interpretation. Several referring expressions can be mapped to the same database token.

Specificity, Definite or Indefinite, and Givenness (Gundel et al. 1993:275) are both named among attributes used for building semantic representations (Byron and Allen 2002:82). The format suggested to describe each RE is:

RE: RE-form
variable
<restrictions on the variable>

where *RE-form* is one of the following:

1. *THE*—The RE is a definite instance NP
2. *A*—The RE is an indefinite instance NP
3. *KIND* —The RE is a bare plural NP

The authors do not discuss mass nouns and abstract nouns.

Suggested output (a final logical term description) of a system implementing this interface after processing the phrase *a truck* would be:

(a x
(and (type x truck)
(refers-to x (elem-of (TRUCK1 TRUCK2 TRUCK3)))))

To evaluate the performance of a system that would implement the proposed interface Byron and Allen (2002:87) manually analyzed a set of dialogs from a medication scheduling domain containing 118 sentences, with 169 REs (disregarding first/second person pronouns). The result achieved was 92% (155 correct semantic representations).

Popescu-Belis (2003) discusses a system for resolving reference in narrative French texts which comprise the first chapter of Balzac's *Le Père Goriot* and the beginning of a short story by Stendhal, *Vittoria Accoramboni*. The author demonstrates how including particular features into analysis affects the overall performance of the system. Popescu-Belis compares several *knowledge sources* and their possible behaviors. Examples of rules composing a behavior would be the rules requiring or blocking the creation of a new referent, or rules that determine compatibility between a referring expression and an entity.

REs are expressions that are bound to entities of a mental space. Such entities can be material or conceptual objects, reified events, relations and properties. The binding between entities and REs in both the mind of the sender and of the receiver involves mental representations of the entities (MRs). The sender generates an RE in order to activate the receiver's MR corresponding to the referent of that RE. Thus reference involves an entity, a sender MR, a receiver MR and an RE in the discourse. The relation between an MR and the entity it represents is usually called specification (Sidner 1981:218). An RE refers via the corresponding MR to the entity specified by the MR.

An MR can be viewed as a collection of REs that are considered to refer to the same entity. Processing an RE amounts to either creating a new MR or attaching the RE to an existing MR. The data structure for an MR can have the following fields:

- *MR.Index_Number*
- *MR.Activation*—a number modeling the contextual salience of the MR
- *MR.List_Of_REs*—the REs that activated the MR
- *MR.List_Of_Characteristic_REs*—a subset of the former, storing the REs that will be used for comparisons later, in the order of their appearance in the discourse.

Figure 2.3: Suggested data structure for a Meaning Representation (MR) (Popescu-Belis 2003:290).

Semantic representations for REs are inferred from the parse tree and its labels. To resolve reference in cases when synonyms or hyponyms are used,

Popescu-Belis built a small network (about 50 words) involving the main concepts of the *Vittoria Accoramboni* text. Therefore the results for that text were better than those for the excerpt from *Le Père Goriot*. The proposed algorithm examines the REs sequentially. For each RE it attempts to determine whether the RE evokes a known or a new MR. In the former case the corresponding MR is retrieved and the current RE is attached to it:

```
For each REi of the text
    For each MRk of the working memory
        For each characteristic REj of MRk
            Find compatibility REi ↔ REj            ← (1)
        Infer compatibility REi ↔ MRk               ← (2)
    Decide if a new MR must be created with REi     ← (3)
    If not, decide to which MRx REi is attached     ← (4)
    Update MRx.list_Of_Characteristic_REs           ← (5), (6)
    Update activation of the MRs                    ← (7)
    Update working memory                           ← (8)
```

Figure 2.4: The reference resolution algorithm (Popescu-Belis 2003:290).

The arrows in Figure 2.4 show the insertion points of the knowledge sources:

1. referring compatibility between two REs
2. referring compatibility between an RE and a MR—a heuristic to determine whether an RE may evoke a given MR or not, based on compatibility of the RE with the REs that characterize the MR
3. creation/attachment—rules that decide between creation of a new MR and attachment to an existing one
4. attach the RE to the most recent among the most active compatible MRs
5. options for the size and the rules for adding or deleting an RE
6. include/exclude pronouns
7. activation—the rules that determine activation of REs
8. rules for adjusting the size of working memory.

Popescu-Belis analyzes how information from these sources affects the performance of the system. In particular, he demonstrates that excluding the rule for referring compatibility between REs significantly reduces the performance of the system. The compatibility rule is formulated as follows:

Two REs may evoke the same MR if:

- they have the same gender

- they have the same number
- they have compatible semantic contents (the head nouns of the REs are duplicates, synonyms, or the second is a hypernym of the first)

Only two very simple rules related to definiteness were considered:

- force the attachment of each definite RE to an existing MR
- force the creation of an MR for each indefinite RE

Implementing these requirements did not improve the performance. The author remarks: "…these scores confirm that the links between definiteness and reference are subtler than the present rules" (Popescu-Belis 2003:297). Overall, the system proposed by Popescu-Belis achieves up to 91% of correct results.

• CHAPTER THREE •

On the Concept of Definiteness

3.1 Selected Ontology

To describe all uses of articles we would need an ontology like the one presented in Russell and Norvig (2003:323–341). Categories are viewed as sets (or more complex objects, that have the *Member* and *Subset* relations defined for them). Membership in a category is based on possessing certain properties, e.g.

$$Orange(x) \wedge Round(x) \wedge Diameter(x) = 9.5" \wedge x \in Balls \Rightarrow x \in Basketballs$$

$$x \in Basketballs \Rightarrow Round(x)$$

Since sets are not physical objects, Russell and Norvig propose to use the term *bunch* to denote several objects as a whole. The definition of a *bunch* that we shall be using in our study is presented at the end of this section. Membership in a set implies being part of a bunch:

$$\forall x\; x \in s \Rightarrow PartOf(x, BunchOf(s))$$

Categories corresponding to mass nouns are also best thought of as sets of objects, whose definitions include only intrinsic properties (like color, density, but not shape or weight). To represent the fact that any part of a butter-object is also a butter-object one could write:

$$x \in Butter \wedge PartOf(y, x) \Rightarrow y \in Butter$$

PhysicalObjects are a subset of *GeneralizedEvents*. The latter are composed from aspects of some piece of the four-dimensional universe. Space-time can be divided into subevents (*SubEvent* is a special case of the *PartOf* relation), and *In* is used when one event's spatial projection is *PartOf* another's, e.g.

$$\exists\, w \quad w \in \mathit{CivilWars} \wedge \mathit{SubEvent}(w, 1640s) \\ \wedge\ \mathit{In}\ (\mathit{Location}\ (w), \mathit{England})$$

For our purposes we would require that a *bunch* consist of at least two members of the same category, which is always the case for categories corresponding to mass nouns. As indicated above, in Russell and Norvig (2003:323) an object is defined simply as a member of a category. We shall be using the term object to refer only to a member of a category that does not consist of other members of the same category. It turns out that practically all cases of the use of articles can be described as depending only on two factors:

1. whether the referent of the noun is an object or a bunch;
2. whether the hearer already knows about its existence in a mental space.

3.2 A Set of Rules for the Use of the Articles

Since we are concerned only with nominal reference, a mental space (MS) can be viewed as a collection of its elements structured by frames. An entity is added to an MS either if it is a default element of an activated frame, or if it was explicitly introduced in the discourse. Each element that can be the referent of a noun *N* is expected to possess all the necessary and sufficient properties of the concept *N*. It can also be assigned some other—secondary—properties *ab* (e.g. expressed by adjectives). The referent of the expression *(ab)N* can only be an object or a bunch and this does not depend on whether *N* is in the singular or plural. An object is an element of an MS with properties *(ab)N* which does not contain two or more parts, each of which also has properties *(ab)N*.

The following set of rules appears to be sufficient for English and German:

<table>
<tr><td>1</td><td colspan="2">Both the speaker and the hearer know that there exists an object with properties (ab)N in the MS and there is only one such object there</td><td>the/der (ab)N</td></tr>
<tr><td>2</td><td colspan="2">The speaker informs the hearer about the existence of one object with properties (ab)N in the MS</td><td>a/ein (ab)N</td></tr>
<tr><td>3</td><td rowspan="3">Both the speaker and the hearer know that there exists a bunch with properties (ab)N in the MS and</td><td>the referent of the noun is one object with properties (ab)N, part of the original bunch</td><td>a/ein (ab)N</td></tr>
<tr><td>4</td><td>the referent of the noun is a bunch with properties (ab)N, part of the original bunch</td><td>Ø (ab)N</td></tr>
<tr><td>5</td><td>the referent of the noun is the original bunch as a whole</td><td>the/der (ab)N</td></tr>
<tr><td>6</td><td colspan="2">The speaker informs the hearer about the existence of a bunch with properties (ab)N in the MS</td><td>Ø (ab)N</td></tr>
<tr><td>7</td><td colspan="2">A noun denotes itself as a sequence of sounds or letters</td><td>Ø (ab)N</td></tr>
<tr><td>8</td><td colspan="2">A noun denotes a subordinate referent (defined below)</td><td>Ø (ab)N</td></tr>
</table>

Figure 3.1: A set of rules that describe the system of articles in English and German.

We believe that referents of proper nouns and words like Eg. *church* or *hospital* meet all requirements needed for a noun to be used with the definite article. Proper nouns are used with the definite article in some Romance languages and even in some dialects of German. The use of the definite vs. zero article with *hospital* varies in British and in American English. Since such words very seldom refer to indefinite entities, the definite article in corresponding noun phrases seems to be redundant.

In the following example we see a zero article in a German sentence, but not in its English translation:

(3.1) *Der Führer wurde noch ein wenig aufgehalten*
durch eine Frau, die...
sich jetzt auf   *Deck zeigte (Kafka 1990: 64).*
ZERO-ART

(3.2) *The pilot was still further detained by a woman who...*
now appeared on   *the deck of the boat (Kafka 1971: 226).*
DEF-ART

Yet *deck* can be used with the zero article in English as well, e.g. in the command:

(3.3) All Hands on Deck!

Rule 7 is known as *material supposition*. Ockham in *Summa Logicae* (1984:93) wrote:

> Material supposition occurs when a term does not supposit significatively but supposits for an utterance or for an inscription. This is clear in 'Man is a name'. 'Man' supposits for itself... Likewise, in the proposition 'Man is written' the supposition can be material, because the term supposits for what is written.

The referent of *N2* in

DEF-ART N1 is INDEF-ART N2
(The N1 ist an N2 / Der N1 ist ein N2)

is the same object as the referent of *N1*, but from a different point of view. The object *N1* has been assigned to a new category. The speaker states that *N1* has not only the sufficient and necessary properties of the concept *N1* (which is a prerequisite for referring to it using the noun *N1*), but also the sufficient and necessary properties of the concept *N2*. In German, where a different construction *(DEF-ART N1 is ZERO-ART N2)* is common, the use of *DEF-ART N1 is INDEF-ART N2* can have a stylistic effect. In the sentence

(3.4) Ich bin Deutscher
I am ZERO-ART German

the role of *Deutscher* 'German' is close to that of an adjective:

(3.5) Wo wohnen Sie? – Ich wohne in Berlin.
Where live you? I live in Berlin.
Welche Nationalität haben Sie? –
Which nationality have you?
Ich bin Deutscher.
I am ZERO-ART German

while the much less frequent

(3.6) Ich bin ein Deutscher.
I am INDEF-ART German.

puts emphasis on the characteristics of the concept *a German person*:

(3.7) *Ich bin ein Deutscher aus Dresden in Sachsen.*
I am INDEF-ART German from Dresden in Saxony.
Mich lässt die Heimat nicht fort... (Kästner 1950:56).
Me lets DEF-ART homeland not away

In English the zero article is possible in such constructions only when the referent of the noun is unique. Fillmore (1988:40) uses the term Unique-Role Nominal Predicate Construction to describe predicate NPs in sentences like:

(3.8) *I was chairman of the committee.*
ZERO-ART

(3.9) *She is chief surgeon to the royal family.*
ZERO-ART

(3.10) *You are now president of the club.*
ZERO-ART

An article is required if the NP is not the predicate of the sentence, or if the referent is not unique. Thus the following sentences are unacceptable:

(3.11) **President of the club resigned.*

(3.12) **She is member of the club.*

We call a *subordinate referent* the set of the properties of a concept which is considered to be a part of or an addition to another set of properties:

(3.13) *Ein Mann in blauem Kittel*
INDEF-ART man in ZERO-ART blue blouse
stieg ans Land (Kafka 1990:64).
climbed ashore

(3.14) *Der Mann verließ mit gesenktem Kopf*
DEF-ART man left with ZERO-ART lowered head
das Zimmer.
DEF-ART room.

Abstract nouns usually express properties of other objects and therefore tend to be used as subordinate referents with a zero article. Yet their referents can also be introduced as independent entities and then the usual rules apply.

In German abstract nouns are used with a definite or indefinite article much more frequently than in English, but historically such use is a relatively late development:

(3.15) *Es war klar, daß eine gewisse Animosität*
It was clear that INDEF-ART certain animosity
des Contadino gegen das studierte
of Contadino against DEF-ART educated
Familienmitglied sich hier Luft machte,
family member demonstrated itself here,
obgleich... Sor Alfo die Bewunderung
althought... Sor Alfo DEF-ART admiration
aller Manardis für den Advokaten teilte (Mann 1955:290).
of all Manardis for DEF-ART advocate shared.

(3.16) *...mir schien, daß er die Gelegenheit wahrnahm, über*
to me appeared, that he DEF-ART oportunity saw, over
die Herrlichkeit der Naturerscheinung selber...
DEF-ART greatness of DEF-ART phenomenon itself...
zu lachen (Mann 1955:292).
to laugh.

(3.17) *"Ich danke Ihnen, liebe Frau, für Ihr Verständnis!" Er habe...*
"I thank you, dear lady, for your sympathy!" He has...
das Verständnis gemeint
DEF-ART sympathy meant
für die Eltern (Mann 1955:284).
with DEF-ART parents.

Mental spaces built on the basis of frames contain objects only in quantities necessary for processes being described. This answers questions like 'Why is it one door?' or 'Which door is meant?' in sentences like following:

(3.18) *When meeting a blind or partially sighted person, the*
driver must not simply wait outside, but should
knock on the door,
DEF-ART
or enter the premises, to announce
his or her arrival (DPTAC 2003).

An article becomes most informative when a speaker in the description of an MS unknown to the hearer mentions an object *N* for the first time. A definite article before *N* shows the hearer that this object lies in the MS of a frame that stipulates the existence of one such object. In this case the definite article before a noun confirms a frame via the object denoted by the noun. This fact can be used by a computer to learn which objects may form frames directly from a text. We discuss an example of such use of the definite article in the next section.

3.3 Analysis of Data from Modern German and English

In this section we demonstrate application of the proposed rules to larger text fragments. The referent of each noun is characterized with respect to its mental space (s) and the rule (r) that determines the choice of an article:

Gehirne (Benn 1990:83–87)
Brains

1. Jetzt saß er auf einem Eckplatz
Now sat he on INDEF-ART corner seat
[s Journey, r 3]
und sah in die Fahrt.
and looked in [the direction of] DEF-ART ride
[s Journey, r 1]
2. Es geht also durch Weinland, besprach er sich,
it goes now through Wine Country, told he himself,
ziemlich flaches, vorbei an Scharlachfeldern,
quite flat, past ZERO-ART scarlet red fields,
[s Rural Landscape, r 6]
die rauchen von Mohn.
which smell of ZERO-ART poppy.
[s Rural Landscape, r 6]
3. Männer arbeiteten im Heu...
ZERO-ART men worked in DEF-ART hay
[s Rural Landscape, r 6] [s Rural Landscape, r 5]
eine Stadt und ein Wagen
INDEF-ART town and INDEF-ART car
[s Journey, r 2] [s Journey, r 2]

über *Berge* *vor* *ein Haus.*
across ZERO-ART mountains bofore INDEF-ART house.
[s Journey, r 6] [s Journey, r 2]

Rönne's journey ends in a place, where, among other things, there are *patios, halls and garages:*

4. *Veranden, Hallen und Remisen,*
ZERO-ART patios, halls and garages,
auf *der Höhe* *eines Gebirges,*
on DEF-ART height of INDEF-ART hill
in *einen Wald* *gebaut –*
into INDEF-ART forest built

The following words establish a connection between these objects and add new elements to the MS, which becomes the space of an instantiated frame. Particularly interesting is the definite article before the noun referring to an element of the MS mentioned for the first time—*Chefarzt* 'chief physician'. It was unclear, up to this point, which frame formed the basis for the current MS. The definite article in *den Chefarzt* suggests that the current MS is a frame which has exactly one chief physician, i.e. a Hospital:

heir wollte Rönne *den Chefarzt*
here wanted Rönne as DEF-ART chief physician
ein paar Wochen *vertreten...*
a pair of weeks act...

The corresponding rules are as follows:

4. *Veranden, Hallen und Remisen,*
ZERO-ART patios, halls and garages,
[s Hospital, r 6]
auf *der Höhe* *eines Gebirges,*
on DEF-ART hight of INDEF-ART hill
[s Hill, r 1] [s Hospital, r 2]
in *einen Wald* *gebaut –*
into INDEF-ART forest built
[s Hospital, r 2]
hier wollte Rönne *den Chefarzt*
here wanted Rönne as DEF-ART chief physician
[s Hospital, r 1]

ein paar Wochen vertreten...
a pair of weeks act...
5. *Die Anstalt lag hoch;*
DEF-ART institution lay high;
[s Hospital, r 1]
Rönne war feierlich zu Mute;
Rönne felt celebratory;
umleuchtet von seiner Einsamkeit
illuminated by his loneleness
besprach er mit den Schwestern
discussed he with DEF-ART nurses
[s Hospital, r 5]
die dienstlichen Angelegenheiten fern und kühl.
DEF-ART business matters aloof and coldly.
[s Hospital, r 5]

The frame Hospital is followed by the frame X-ray Examination:

6. *Er überließ ihnen alles zu tun:*
He let them do everything:
das Herumdrehen der Hebel,
DEF-ART turning DEF-ART levers,
[s X-ray Examination, r 1] [s X-ray Examination, r 5]
das Befestigen der Lampen,
DEF-ART fastening DEF-ART lamps,
[s X-ray Examination, r 1] [s X-ray Examination, r 5]
den Antrieb der Motore.
DEF-ART starting DEF-ART motors.
[s X-ray Examination, r 1] [s X-ray Examination, r 5]
7. *Dann nahm er selber seine Hände,*
Then took he himself his hands,
führte sie über die Röntgenröhre,
moved them over DEF-ART Roentgen pipes,
[s X-ray Examination, r 5]
verschob das Quecksilber der Quarzlampe.
adjusted DEF-ART quicksilver of DEF-ART quartz lamp.
[s X-ray Examination, r 5] [s X-ray Examination, r 1]

After this another frame appears in the story. One man is singled out of *die Aussichtslosen* 'DEF-ART hopeless patients'. First denoted by *ein solcher* 'one such'—as an element of the frame Hospital—he is later described in the context of the frame Terminal Patient. Some elements of the latter are mentioned before *ein solcher*. Thus in the part of the story below nouns refer to elements of two alternating frames:

1. *die Anstalt* 'DEF-ART institution',
   die Aussichtslosen 'DEF-ART hopeless patients',
   ein solcher 'one such';

2. *die Schreibereien und der Schmutz*
   'DEF-ART paperwork and DEF-ART dirt',
   der Tod 'DEF-ART death',
   die Kur 'DEF-ART treatment',
   die Schmerzen 'DEF-ART pains',
   die Genesung 'DEF-ART convalescence',
   das Blut 'DEF-ART blood' ,
   der Hals 'DEF-ART throat'.

8. Es war in der Anstalt üblich,
It was in DEF-ART institution common,
[s Hospital, r 1]
die Aussichtslosen unter Verschleierung dieses Tatbestandes
DEF-ART hopeless [patients] without revealing that fact
[s Hospital, r 5]
in ihre Familien zu entlassen
to their families to release
wegen der Schreibereien und des Schmutzes,
because of DEF-ART paperwork and DEF-ART dirt,
[s Terminal Patient, r 5] [s Terminal Patient, r 5]
den der Tod mit sich bringt.
which DEF-ART death with itself brings.
[s Terminal Patient, r 5]
9. Auf einen solchen trat Rönne zu,
One such [patient] met Rönne
beglückwünschte ihn zu der gelungenen Kur
congratulated him on DEF-ART successful treatment
[s Terminal Patient, r 1]
und sah ihm nach, wie er von dannen trottete.
and watched him, as he away trotted.
10. Er wird nun nach Hause gehen, dachte Rönne,
He will now go home, thought Rönne,

die Schmerzen als *eine lästige* *Begleiterscheinung*
DEF-ART pains as INDEF-ART annoying side effect
[s Terminal Patient, r 5] [s Terminal Patient, r 2]
der Genesung *empfinden...*
of DEF-ART convalescence perceiving...
[s Terminal Patient, r 1]
bis *die Nacht kommt*
until DEF-ART night comes
[s Terminal Patient, r 1]
mit *dem Blut* *im Hals.*
with DEF-ART blood in DEF-ART throat.
[s Terminal Patient, r 5] [s Terminal Patient, r 1]

Below is the beginning of a short story by Kafka. After the text fragment we shall discuss the mental spaces that contain the referents of the nouns and the use of articles in the fragment.

Der Jäger Gracchus (Kafka 1990:63–65)
The Hunter Grachhus

1. *Zwei Knaben saßen*
ZERO-ART two boys were sitting
[s Harbor, r 6]
auf *der Quaimauer und*
on DEF-ART harbor wall
[s Harbor, r 1]
spielten *Würfel.*
playing with ZERO-ART dice
[s Harbor, r 6]
2. *Ein Mann* *las* *eine Zeitung*
INDEF-ART man was reading INDEF-ART newspaper
[s Harbor, r 2] [s Harbor, r 2]
auf *den Stufen* *eines Denkmals*
on DEF-ART steps of INDEF-ART monument
[s Monument, r 5] [s Harbor, r 2]
im Schatten *des säbelschwingenden Helden.*
in DEF-ART shadow of DEF-ART hero flourishing his sword.
[s Monument, r 1] [s Monument, r 1]
3. *Ein Obstverkäufer* *lag neben seiner Ware*
INDEF-ART fruit-seller was lying beside his wares
[s Harbor, r 2]

und blickte auf den See hinaus.
and gazing at DEF-ART sea.
[s Harbor, r 1]
4. In der Tiefe einer Kneipe sah man
At DEF-ART back of INDEF-ART café one could see
[s Cafe, r 1] [s Harbor, r 2]
durch die leeren Tür- und Fensterlöcher
through DEF-ART empty window and door openings
[s Cafe, r 5]
zwei Männer beim Wein.
ZERO-ART two men drinking DEF-ART wine.
[s Cafe, r 6] [s Cafe, r 5]
5. Der Wirt saß vorn
DEF-ART proprietor was sitting in front
[s Cafe, r 1]
an einem Tisch und schlummerte.
at INDEF-ART table and dozing.
[s Cafe, r 3]
6. Eine Barke schwebte leise,
INDEF-ART bark was moving silently
[s Harbor, r 2]
als werde sie über dem Wasser getragen,
as if it over DEF-ART water were borne
[s Harbor, r 5]
in den kleinen Hafen.
to DEF-ART little harbor.
[s Harbor, r 1]
7. Ein Mann in blauem Kittel
INDEF-ART man in ZERO-ART blue blouse
[s Harbor, r 2] [s Harbor, r 8]
stieg ans Land
climbed to DEF-ART land
[s Harbor, r 1]
und zog die Seile durch die Ringe.
and drew DEF-ART ropes through DEF-ART rings.
[s Bark, r 5] [s Bark, r 5]
8. Zwei andere Männer
ZERO-ART two other men
[s Harbor, r 6]

in dunklen Röcken
in ZERO-ART dark coats
[s Harbor, r 8]
mit Silberknöpfen
with ZERO-ART silver buttons
[s Harbor, r 6]
trugen hinter dem Bootsmann eine Bahre, auf der
carried behind DEF-ART boatman INDEF-ART bier, on which
[s Harbor, r 1] [s Harbor, r 2]
unter einem großen
beneath INDEF-ART large
[s Harbor, r 2]
blumengemusterten, gefransten Seidentuch
flower-patterned fringed silk cloth
offenbar ein Mensch lag.
apparently INDEF-ART man was lying
[s Harbor, r 2]
9. Auf dem Quai kümmerte sich
On DEF-ART quay troubled
[s Harbor, r 1]
niemand um die Ankömmlinge,
nobody about DEF-ART newcomers,
[s Harbor, r 5]
selbst als sie die Bahre niederstellten,
even when they DEF-ART bier lowered,
[s Harbor, r 1]
um auf den Bootsführer zu warten,
in order for DEF-ART boatman to wait,
[s Bark, r 1]
der noch an den Seilen arbeitete,
who still with DEF-ART ropes was busy,
[s Bark, r 5]
trat niemand heran,
went nobody nearer,
niemand richtete eine Frage an sie,
nobody directed INDEF-ART question at them,
[s Harbor, r 2]
niemand sah sie genauer an.
nobody looked at them with interest.

10. Der Führer wurde noch ein wenig aufgehalten
DEF-ART pilot was a little longer detained
[s Bark, r 1]
durch eine Frau,
by INDEF-ART woman
[s Bark, r 2]
die mit aufgelösten Haaren
who with ZERO-ART loosened hair
[s Bark, r 8]
sich jetzt auf Deck zeigte.
now on ZERO-ART deck appeared.
[idiomatic]
11. Dann kam er, wies auf
Then came he, pointed at
ein gelbliches, zweistöckiges Haus,
INDEF-ART yellowish two-storeyed house
[s Harbor, r 2]
das sich links nahe beim Wasser geradlinig erhob,
which on the left nearby at DEF-ART water abruptly rose,
[s Harbor, r 5]
die Träger nahmen die Last auf,
DEF-ART bearers lifted DEF-ART burden
[s Harbor, r 5] [s Harbor, r 1]
und trugen sie durch das niedrige,
and carried it throught DEF-ART low
[s House, r 1]
aber von schlanken Säulen gebildete Tor.
but by ZERO-ART graceful pillars formed gate.
[s House, r 6]
12. Ein kleiner Junge öffnete ein Fenster,
INDEF-ART little boy opened INDEF-ART window
[s House, r 2] [s House, r 3]
bemerkte noch gerade, wie der Trupp
noticed just in time how DEF-ART party
[s House, r 1]
im Haus verschwand,
in DEF-ART house vanished
[s House, r 1]

und schloß wieder eilig das Fenster.
and shut again hastily DEF-ART window.
[s House, r 1]
13. Auch das Tor wurde nun geschlossen.
Also DEF-ART gate was now shut.
[s House, r 1]
14. Ein Taubenschwarm, der bisher
INDEF-ART flock of doves which until now
[s House, r 2]
den Glockenturm umflogen hatte,
around DEF-ART belfry had been flying
[s House, r 1]
ließ sich jetzt vor dem Hause nieder.
alighted before DEF-ART house.
[s House, r 1]
15. Als werde im Hause ihre Nahrung aufbewahrt,
As if in DEF-ART house their food were stored
[s House, r 1]
sammelten sich die Tauben vor dem Tor.
assembled DEF-ART doves in front of DEF-ART gate.
[s The House, r 5] [s House, r 1]
16. Eine flog bis zum ersten Stock auf
one of them flew up to DEF-ART first floor
[s House, r 1]
und pickte an die Fensterscheibe.
and pecked at DEF-ART windowpane.
[s House, r 1]
17. Es waren hellfarbige wohlgepflegte, lebhafte Tiere.
Those were ZERO-ART bright-hued well-tended lively birds.
[s House, r 6]
18. In großem Schwung
In ZERO-ART wide sweep
[s Bark, r 8]
warf ihnen die Frau
flung to them DEF-ART woman
[s Bark, r 1]
aus der Barke Körner hin,
from DEF-ART bark ZERO-ART grain,
[s Bark, r 1] [s Bark, r 6]

die sammelten sie auf und flogen dann
they picked it up and flew then
zu der Frau hinüber.
to DEF-ART woman over.
[s Bark, r 1]
19. Ein Mann, im Zylinderhut
INDEF-ART man in DEF-ART top hat
[s Harbor, r 2] [s Clothing, r 1]
mit Trauerband
with ZERO-ART mourning stripe
[s Man, r 8]
kam eines der schmalen, stark abfallenden Gäßchen,
descended one of DEF-ART narrow, steep streets
[s Harbor, r 5]
die zum Hafen führten, herab.
which to DEF-ART harbor led.
[s Harbor, r 1]
20. Er blickte aufmerksam umher, alles bekümmerte ihn.
He glanced vigilantly around, everything distressed him.
21. Auf den Stufen des Denkmals
On DEF-ART steps of DEF-ART monument
[s Monument, r 5] [s Monument, r 1]
lagen Obstschalen.
were lying ZERO-ART fruit skins
[s Monument, r 6]
22. An der Stubentür klopfte er an,
At DEF-ART house door knocked he,
[s House, r 1]
gleichzeitig nahm er den Zylinderhut
at the same time took he DEF-ART top hat
[s Clothing, r 1]
in seine schwarzbehandschuhte Rechte.
with his black-gloved right hand.
23. Gleich wurde geöffnet,
At once [the door] was opened
wohl fünfzig kleine Knaben bildeten
ZERO-ART around fifty little boys formed
[s House, r 6]

ein Spalier *im langen Flurgang*
INDEF-ART guard of honor in DEF-ART long entry hall
[s House, r 2] [s House, r 1]
und verbeugten sich.
and bowed.

The referents of most of the nouns in the fragment lie in one of the three mental spaces: Harbor, Bark, and House. Below we listed entities from each mental space which are either

1. elements of frames introduced with a definite article, or
2. elements of mental spaces referred to several times.

In both cases the definite article helps to identify the mental space that contains the referent of a noun (cf. Chap. 4). For each entity we provide corresponding fragments of sentences from the text. In parenthesis before each sentence fragment we put its number in the text followed by letter 'r' (for repeat).

MS HARBOR

Harbor Wall

(1 r) Zwei Knaben saßen
ZERO-ART two boys were sitting
[s Harbor, r 6]
auf der Quaimauer...
on DEF-ART harbor wall
[s Harbor, r 1]

Monument

(2 r) Ein Mann las eine Zeitung
INDEF-ART man was reading INDEF-ART newspaper
auf den Stufen eines Denkmals...
on DEF-ART steps of INDEF-ART monument...
[s Harbor, r 2]

(21 r) Auf den Stufen des Denkmals
On DEF-ART steps of DEF-ART monument
[s Monument, r 1]

lagen *Obstschalen*
were lying ZERO-ART fruit skins

Sea

(3 r) *Ein Obstverkäufer...*
INDEF-ART fruit-seller…
blickte auf den See hinaus.
gazing at DEF-ART sea.
[s Harbor, r 1]

Harbor

(6 r) *Eine Barke schwebte leise...*
INDEF-ART bark was moving silently…
in den kleinen Hafen.
to DEF-ART little harbor.
[s Harbor, r 1]

(19 r) *Ein Mann... kam eines*
INDEF-ART man… descended one of
der schmalen, stark abfallenden Gäßchen,
DEF-ART narrow, steep streets
die zum Hafen führten, herab.
which to DEF-ART harbor led.
[s Harbor, r 1]

Quay

(9 r) *Auf dem Quai kümmerte sich*
On DEF-ART quay troubled
[s Harbor, r 1]
niemand um die Ankömmlinge...
nobody about DEF-ART newcomers…

House

(11 r) *Dann kam er, wies auf*
Then came he, pointed at

ein gelbliches, zweistöckiges Haus...
INDEF-ART yellowish two-storeyed house
[s Harbor, r 2]

Water

(11 r) Dann kam er, wies auf
Then came he, pointed at
ein gelbliches, zweistöckiges Haus,
INDEF-ART yellowish two-storeyed house
das sich links nahe
which on the left nearby
beim Wasser geradlinig erhob...
at DEF-ART water abruptly rose
[s Harbor, r 5]

MS BARK

Ropes

(7 r) Ein Mann in blauem Kittel
INDEF-ART man in ZERO-ART blue blouse
stieg ans Land
climbed to DEF-ART land
und zog die Seile durch die Ringe.
and drew DEF-ART ropes through DEF-ART rings.
[s Bark, r 5]

(9 r) ...um auf den Bootsführer zu warten,
in order for DEF-ART boatman to wait,
der noch an den Seilen arbeitete...
who still with DEF-ART ropes was busy
[s Bark, r 5]

Boatman

(9 r) als sie die Bahre niederstellten,
when they DEF-ART bier lowered,
um auf den Bootsführer zu warten...
so as for DEF-ART boatman to wait
[s Bark, r 1]

(10 r) Der Führer wurde noch ein wenig aufgehalten...
DEF-ART pilot was a little longer detained
[s Bark, r 1]

Woman

(10 r) Der Führer wurde noch ein wenig aufgehalten
DEF-ART pilot was a little longer detained
durch eine Frau...
by INDEF-ART woman
[s Bark, r 2]

(18 r) warf ihnen die Frau
flung to them DEF-ART woman
[s Bark, r 1]
aus der Barke Körner hin...
from DEF-ART bark ZERO-ART grain

MS HOUSE

Gate

(11 r) die Träger nahmen die Last auf,
DEF-ART bearers lifted DEF-ART burden
und trugen sie durch das niedrige,
and carried it throught DEF-ART low
[s House, r 1]
aber von schlanken Säulen gebildete Tor.
but by ZERO-ART graceful pillars formed gate.

(13 r) Auch das Tor wurde nun geschlossen.
Also DEF-ART gate was now shut.
[s House, r 1]

(15 r) Als werde im Hause
As if in DEF-ART house
ihre Nahrung aufbewahrt,
their food were stored
sammelten sich die Tauben
assembled DEF-ART doves

vor *dem Tor.*
in front of DEF-ART gate.
[s House, r 1]

Window

(12 r) Ein kleiner Junge
INDEF-ART little boy
öffnete *ein Fenster ...*
opened INDEF-ART window
[s House, r 3]

(12 r) ... und schloß wieder eilig *das Fenster.*
and shut again hastily DEF-ART window.
[s House, r 1]

House

(12 r) ... bemerkte noch gerade, *wie* *der Trupp*
noticed just in time how DEF-ART party
im Haus verschwand...
in DEF-ART house vanished...
[s House, r 1]

(14 r) Ein Taubenschwarm...
INDEF-ART flock of doves...
ließ sich jetzt vor *dem Hause nieder.*
alighted before DEF-ART house.
[s House, r 1]

(15 r) Als werde *im Hause*
As if in DEF-ART house
[s House, r 1]
ihre Nahrung aufbewahrt,
their food were stored
sammelten sich *die Tauben*
assembled DEF-ART doves
vor *dem Tor.*
in front of DEF-ART gate.

Entry Hall

(23 r) *...wohl fünfzig kleine Knaben bildeten*
ZERO-ART around fifty little boys formed
ein Spalier *im langen Flurgang*
INDEF-ART guard of honor in DEF-ART long entry hall
[s House, r 1]

As we can see, referents of the nouns lie in several alternating mental spaces. References to an element of a particular mental space occur in sentences sometimes separated by entire paragraphs, e.g. Monument in sentences 2 and 21, Harbor in 6 and 19, Woman in 10 and 18. The definite article is a clear indication of coreference in such cases. In Chapter 4 we demonstrate how an automated system uses the articles to determine composition of mental spaces and instances of coreference in a published English translation of the fragment from Kafka above.

We conclude this section with the analysis of a fragment from *The Financier* by Th. Dreiser (1946:81–82). Further analysis of data from Modern English is given in Chapter 4 as part of the description of our algorithm for automated nominal reference resolution.

Chapter X

1. Many excellent and expensive *houses were*
ZERO-ART
[s Town, r 6]
being erected.
2. The front lawn, with some
DEF-ART
[s House, r 1]
attempt at floral gardening,
was achieving local popularity.
3. In *the homes*
DEF-ART
[s Town, r 5]
of *the Tighes, the Leighs, Arthur Rivers, and others,*
DEF-ART
[s Town, r 5]
he had noticed *art objects of some*
ZERO-ART
[s House, r 6]

distinction— *bronzes, marbles,*

ZERO-ART

[s House, r 6]

hangings, pictures, clocks, rugs.

4. It seemed to him now that his comparatively commonplace

house could be made into something charming

and for comparatively little *money.*

ZERO-ART

[s Renovation, r 6]

5. *The dining-room for instance which,*

DEF-ART

[s House, r 1]

through two plain *windows*

ZERO-ART

[s Dining Room, r 6]

set in *a hat side wall back of*

INDEF-ART

[s Dining Room, r 2]

the veranda, looked south over *a stretch*

DEF-ART INDEF-ART

[s House, r 1] [s House, r 2]

of *grass and several trees and bushes*

ZERO-ART

[s House, r 6]

to *a dividing fence where* *the Semple property*

INDEF-ART DEF-ART

[s House, r 2] [s House, r 1]

ended and *a neighbor's began,*

INDEF-ART

[s House, r 2]

could be made so much more attractive.

6. That fence— *sharp-pointed, gray palings—*

ZERO-ART

[s House, r 6]

could be torn away and *a hedge*

INDEF-ART

[s House, r 2]

put in its place.

7. The wall which divided
DEF-ART
[s House, r 1]
the dining-room from *the parlor*
DEF-ART DEF-ART
[s House, r 1] [s House, r 1]
could be knocked through and *a hanging*
INDEF-ART
[s House, r 2]
of some pleasing character put in its place.
8. A bay-window could be built
INDEF-ART
[s House, r 2]
to replace *the two present oblong windows—*
DEF-ART
[s House, r 5]
a bay which would come down
INDEF-ART
[s House, r 2]
to *the floor and open out*
DEF-ART
[s House, r 1]
on *the lawn via*
DEF-ART
[s House, r 1]
swiveled, diamond-shaped, lead-paned frames.
ZERO-ART
[s House, r 6]
9. All this shabby, nondescript furniture, collected from heaven knows where – partly inherited
from *the Semples and the Wiggins and partly bought—could*
DEF-ART
[s Town, r 5]
be thrown out or sold and something better and more harmonious introduced.
10. He knew *a young man*
INDEF-ART
[s Town, r 2]

by *the name of Ellsworth,* *an architect newly*
DEF-ART INDEF-ART
[s Human, r 1] [s Town, r 2]
graduated from *a local school.*
INDEF-ART
[s Town, r 3]
11. When he suggested *the young man to*
DEF-ART
[s Town, r 1]
Lillian, she placidly agreed with him and also with his own ideas of how *the house could be revised.*
DEF-ART
[s House, r 1]
12. So while they were gone on their honeymoon Ellsworth began *the revision*
DEF-ART
[s Renovation, r 1]
on *an estimated cost of*
INDEF-ART
[s Renovation, r 2]
three thousand dollars,
ZERO-ART
[s Renovation, r 6]
including *the furniture.*
DEF-ART
[s Renovation, r 5]
13. It was not completed for nearly *three weeks*
ZERO-ART
[s Renovation, r 6]
after their return; but when finished made
a comparatively new house.
INDEF-ART
[s House, r 2; cf. discussion of the construct *DEF-ART N1 is INDEF-ART N2* in Section 3.2]
14. The dining-room bay hung low over the grass, as Frank
DEF-ART
[s House, r 1]
wished, and *the windows were diamond-paned and leaded,*
DEF-ART
[s House, r 5]

swiveled on *brass rods.*
ZERO-ART
[s House, r 6]
15. *The parlor and dining-room*
DEF-ART
[s House, r 1]
were separated by *sliding doors.*
ZERO-ART
[s House, r 6]
16. *Old English oak was used in*
ZERO-ART
[s Dining Room, r 6]
the dining-room, *an American imitation of*
DEF-ART INDEF-ART
[s House, r 1] [s House, r 2]
Chippendale and Sheraton for *the sitting-room*
DEF-ART
[s House, r 1]
and *the bedrooms.*
DEF-ART
[s House, r 5]

3.4 Evaluation of Results

In this chapter we presented definitions of possible types of referents of a noun based on a modified ontology from Russell and Norvig (2003:323–341). Using the definitions of referent types, a set of eight rules for the use of articles in English and German was formulated. We demonstrated application of the rules to example sentences from both languages, and discussed constructions with an indefinite and zero article in predicate NPs.

Further, we analyzed uses of articles in text fragments from German and English. Every noun with an article was characterized with respect to the mental space of its referent and the rule determining the choice of the article. A larger text fragment usually contains references to elements of several mental spaces which are often interleaved. We have shown that information provided by the articles helps to identify instances of coreference even in cases where references to an element of a mental space are several paragraphs apart.

The proposed approach appears to be adequate in all analyzed cases. Of particular interest are occurrences of the definite article at first mention of default elements of frames. The article confirms that the mental space containing the referent of the noun is an instance of a frame that requires the presence of exactly one member of the corresponding category. More generally, the formulated rules allow us to infer information about the mental space that determined the choice of a particular article. This information can be used for automated reference resolution, which will form the subject of the next chapter.

CHAPTER FOUR

Application of the Concept of Definiteness in a Reference Resolution Algorithm

The nominal reference resolution system that we implemented consists of a parser and an algorithm that uses information expressed by the category of definiteness, as well as a heuristic function for ordering representations of mental spaces.

4.1 A Unification Parser

Our system includes a unification parser (Jurafsky and Martin 2000:418–437), to which we added functionality required for our algorithm. The parser uses rules of the form:

(X → (Y Z)
((0 f1 f2) = (1 f1 f2))
((0 f1 f3) = (2 f1 f3))
((1 f4 f5) = (2 f4 f5)))

where *X, Y* and *Z* are categories in our grammar, *0, 1, 2* are indices of elements in the first line, *f1* through *f5* form features. A feature is a sequence of symbols representing syntactic and semantic categories, e.g. the features of the form *eats* can be formulated as

((head agreement number) = sg)
((head agreement person) = 3)
((head object cat) = NP)
((head sem category) = eat)

The token *head* stands at the beginning to mark the root node of the graph corresponding to a parse; *sem* is the root of the semantic component, the rest of the graph represents syntactic properties; *cat* and *category* refer to categories in the syntactic and semantic components, respectively:

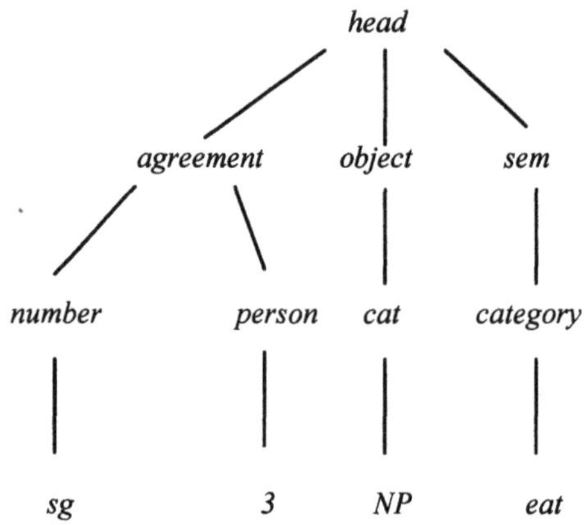

The first line of the rule—

X → *(Y Z)*

consists of one element to the left of the arrow—it represents the resulting category—and of an arbitrarily long list of elements to the right of the arrow representing results of previous unifications. The rest of the rule are expressions with an *equal* sign which can be of two types:

1. expressions setting the value of a feature in the resulting category. Such expressions will have *0* at the beginning on the left hand side, e.g.

   ((0 f1 f2) = (1 f1 f2))

   which means that the feature *(f1 f2)* of the element at index *0*, i.e. *X*, should be set to the value of the feature *(f1 f2)* of the element at index *1 (Y)*. Each sequence in parentheses can be arbitrarily long. If the first element to the right of the arrow has the feature

   ((head agreement number) = pl)

   the second element has the feature

   ((head agreement person) = 3)

and the rule contains expressions

(0 head agreement number) =
(1 head agreement number)
(0 head agreement person) =
(2 head agreement person)

the resulting constituent will have both features:

((head agreement number) = pl)
((head agreement person) = 3)

2. expressions involving only (indices of) elements to the right of the arrow, e.g.

   (1 f4 f5) = (2 f4 f5)

   which means that in order for the whole rule to succeed the values of the feature *(f4 f5)* of *Y* and *Z* should match.

Unification of two sets of features succeeds if the value of every feature present in both sets is the same. The features present only in one of the sets cannot cause unification to fail. The result is the union of two sets. Here is an example from our implementation of the parser. The second and the third lines of our rule for Noun Phrase *NP*

(NP → (D Nnon_max)
((0 head) = (2 head))
((0 head) = (1 head)))

set the *head* feature of the element at index *0* in the first line, i.e. *NP*, to the result of unification of the head features of elements at indices *1* and *2*—*D* and *Nnon_max*. Now if one of the rules for Determiner *D* is

(D → a
((0 head sem definite) = -)
((0 head agreement number) = sg))

and the lexicon entry for *student* is

(Nnon_max → student
((0 head agreement number) = sg)
((0 head sem category) = student)
((0 head sem number) = sg)
((0 head sem bunch) = -))

we shall be able to parse the phrase

a student

because *a* matches the Determiner rule, *student* matches the *Nnon_max* rule and unification required by the rule

NP → (D Nnon_max)

succeeds because the value of the only feature present both in the rule for *D* and *Nnon_max*—

(head agreement number)

is the same. The features present only in one of the components are simply combined during unification for the resulting *NP*, yielding the following set:

(((0 head agreement number) = sg))
((0 head sem category) = student)
((0 head sem number) = sg)
((0 head sem definite) = -)
((0 head sem bunch) = -)))

The presented approach makes it easy to express both syntactic and semantic information, e.g. in order to enforce a particular number of arguments, we implemented the following idea. Verbs have auxiliary *subcat* (for 'subcategorization') features that explicitly form a list whose last element is marked with the token **end**. Parsing is successful only if we reach the end of the list. The rule that forms a *VP* (which we use to represent a maximal projection) is:

(VP → (Vnon_max)
*((1 subcat) = *end*)*
((0 head) = (1 head)))

This rule will be matched, e.g. by *go*, whose lexicon entry has:

(Vnon_max → go
*((0 subcat) = *end*)*
...

A list is a recursive data structure whose first element is marked as *first*, and all other elements as *rest*. A rule that does not produce a maximal projection simply makes a step in the list by setting the *subcat* feature of the resulting *Vnon_max* to the *rest* element of the *subcat* feature of *Vnon_max* on the right hand side of the first line.

(Vnon_max → (Vnon_max NP)
((0 subcat) = (1 subcat rest))
...

To account for cases when particular meanings of a verb can have fewer objects than usual we added the feature *default-steps* to each verb, together with the rule:

(VP → (Vnon_max)
((0 head default-steps) = 1)
*((1 subcat rest) = *end*)*
((0 head) = (1 head)))

This rule requires *default-steps* be *1*, and if that is the case, allows one to create a *VP* one step earlier than the main rule, which instead of

*((1 subcat rest) = *end*)*

has

*((1 subcat) = *end*)*

Putting all together, the rule for the infinitive of an intransitive verb looks like this:

(Vnon_max → go
((0 head default-steps) = 0)
((0 head subject cat) = NP)
((0 head sem category) = go)
((0 head sem agent) = (0 head subject head sem))
*((0 subcat) = *end*))*

while a possible rule for a transitive verb with *0* or *1* objects would be:

(Vnon_max → eat
((0 head default-steps) = 1)
((0 head subject cat) = NP)
((0 head object cat) = NP)
((0 head sem category) = eat)
((0 head sem agent) = (0 head subject head sem))
((0 head sem object) = (0 head object head sem))
*((0 subcat rest) = *end*))*

Regarding Noun Phrases, we would like our parser to discover errors like

(4.1) **Jan gave Lynn apple.*

but allow *apples* or *butter* as the object. Since a category (a set) is not a physical object, in order to denote objects like the referent of *the apples* in

(4.2) *The apples in this bag weigh two pounds.*

a special term, e.g. *bunch* (Russell & Norvig 2003:323–341), is needed. This term was discussed in detail in Section 3.1. The entries for nouns in our lexicon will contain a feature *bunch*, whose value will be '+' if the noun can refer to a bunch and '–' otherwise. The value of *bunch* must be '+' in order for a non-maximal projection to be parsed as an *NP*:

(NP → (Nnon_max)
((1 head sem bunch) = +)
((0 head) = (1 head))
((0 head sem definite) = zero))

This rule introduces the zero article into the representation by setting the value of *(0 head sem definite)*.

For cases when a definite or an indefinite article is present we have the rules:

(NP → (D Nnon_max)
((0 head) = (2 head))
((0 head) = (1 head)))

(D → the
((0 head sem definite) = +))

(D → a
((0 head sem definite) = -)
((0 head agreement number) = sg))

Forming an NP with possessive or demonstrative pronouns also leads to setting the *definite* feature to '+'.

We have also implemented the rule

Nnon_max → AP Nnon_max* Nnon_max*

where *AP* stands for Adjective Phrase and '*' means zero or more instances of an clcmcnt.

Attributes are collected in a list-of-properties:

(Nnon_max → (Nnon_max Nnon max)
((0 head) = (2 head))
((0 head list-of-properties) = (1))
((0 head sem list-of-properties) = (1 head sem)))

(Nnon_max → (AP Nnon_max)
((0 head) = (2 head))
((0 head list-of-properties) = (1))
((0 head sem list-of-properties) = (1 head sem)))

(Nnon_max → (Q Nnon_max)
((0 head) = (2 head))
((0 head quantif) = (1))
((0 head sem quantif) = (1 head sem)))

Parsing the sentence

(4.3) A student read a book yesterday

will produce the following result:

```
([CAT: S]
 [HEAD: (
    [SEM:  ([CATEGORY: READ]
             [AGENT: ([DEFINITE: -] [BUNCH: -]
                      [CATEGORY: STUDENT] [NUMBER: SG])]
             [OBJECT: ([DEFINITE: -] [BUNCH: -]
                      [CATEGORY: BOOK] [NUMBER: SG])]
             [ADV-PHRASE: ([CATEGORY: YESTERDAY])] )]
    [SUBJECT: ([CAT: NP]
               [HEAD: ([CAT: N]
                       [AGREEMENT: ([NUMBER: SG] [PERSON: 3])]
                       [SEM: ([DEFINITE: -]
                              [BUNCH: -]
                              [CATEGORY: STUDENT]
                              [NUMBER: SG])])] )]
    [OBJECT: ([CAT: NP]
              [HEAD: ([CAT: N]
                      [AGREEMENT: ([NUMBER: SG])]
                      [SEM: ([DEFINITE: -]
                      [BUNCH: -]
                      [CATEGORY: BOOK]
                      [NUMBER: SG])])]  )]
    [ADV-PHRASE: ([CAT: ADV-PHRASE]
                  [HEAD: ([SEM: ([CATEGORY: YESTERDAY])] )] )] )])
```

From such parses, our system extracts lists of features corresponding to all nouns in the current sentence, preserving the order in which they appear:

(parse-nouns '(a student read a book yesterday)) →
(("student" (NUMBER SG) (DEFINITE -) (BUNCH -))
("book" (NUMBER SG) (DEFINITE -) (BUNCH -)))

(parse-nouns '(the waiter sat us at a terrible table)) →
(("waiter" (NUMBER SG) (DEFINITE +) (BUNCH -))
("table" (NUMBER SG) (DEFINITE -) (BUNCH -)))

(parse-nouns '(the pilot was still further detained by a woman
who now appeared with loosened hair on the deck
of the boat)) →
(("pilot" (NUMBER SG) (DEFINITE +) (BUNCH -))
("woman" (NUMBER SG) (DEFINITE -) (BUNCH -))
("hair" (NUMBER SG) (DEFINITE ZERO) (BUNCH +))
("deck" (NUMBER SG) (DEFINITE +) (BUNCH -))
("boat" (NUMBER SG) (DEFINITE +) (BUNCH -)))

In Section 4.3 we shall describe some additional features used by the parser.

4.2 A Heuristic for Ordering Known Spaces

In the process of reference resolution, our system uses a heuristic function that, given a noun that is currently being processed by the system and a list of nouns representing already known mental spaces, orders the latter by likelihood of association with the current noun. FIND-CLOSEST uses co-occurrence counts in a large untagged corpus. The function takes in two arguments, a noun *n* and a list of nouns *W*. It returns a normalized list of values for each element of *W*. For convenience, we insert the noun with the highest score at the front of the result:

(find-closest "door" '("house" "face" "war" "sea")) →
("house" 0.5167507 0.29620022 0.057632707 0.12941638)

(find-closest "eye" '("house" "face" "war" "sea")) →
("face" 0.20473619 0.56622374 0.03303618 0.1960039)

There are several known approaches and tools for achieving such functionality, e.g. the Latent Semantic Analysis (LSA) kit. We used our own implementation which is presented in Appendix B.

4.3 The Algorithm for Nominal Reference Resolution

This section describes how the components discussed earlier—the parser, the heuristic function and the rules for the use of determiners—are combined in a system for nominal reference resolution.

In addition to the regular features, nouns that are likely to be indicators of an instantiated frame are marked in the lexicon as *possible-frame-ref.* Such nouns include, for example, *house, restaurant, ship.* A full rule looks like this:

(Nnon_max → house
((0 head agreement number) = sg)
((0 head sem number) = sg)
((0 head sem category) = house)
((0 head sem bunch) = -)
((0 head sem frame-ref) = possible-frame-ref))

Thus from the parse of the sentence

(4.4) *Peter Blood smoked a pipe in his house and tended the geraniums boxed on the sill of his window.*

we will extract the following list of features:

(("peter-blood" (NUMBER SG) (DEFINITE +) (BUNCH -))
("pipe" (NUMBER SG) (DEFINITE -) (BUNCH -))
("house" (NUMBER SG) (DEFINITE +)
(BUNCH -) POSSIBLE-FRAME-REF)
("geranium" (NUMBER PL) (DEFINITE +) (BUNCH +))
("sill" (NUMBER SG) (DEFINITE +) (BUNCH -))
("window" (NUMBER SG) (DEFINITE +) (BUNCH -)))

Lexicon entries for nouns marked as *possible-frame-ref* can also contain one or two nouns that describe most important elements of the frame. This improves the results of reference resolution in case of direct matches, and makes the performance of the heuristic function more robust. The corresponding tag is *frame-add*, e.g.

(harbor (NUMBER SG) (DEFINITE +) (BUNCH -)
POSSIBLE-FRAME-REF (FRAME-ADD (sea)))

Some lexicon entries contain a short list of synonyms and hypernyms. The lexicon used by our system can be created automatically using general synonym/hyponym dictionaries and broad-coverage tools for frame analysis (e.g. FrameNet).

Next we present a general description of our algorithm for nominal reference resolution. The pseudocode for all its major functions is provided in Appendix A.

1	Parse a sentence, put lists of features (LFs) representing all encountered nouns in a buffer. Repeat this until the first LF marked as *possible-frame-ref* is encountered (a significant number of nouns in the dictionary, which can be domain-specific, is expected to have this property. The frame World can be used as a default initial MS). After the first frame is determined, process the contents of the buffer at the end of each sentence; empty the buffer after each iteration.
2	Move LFs containing the tag *possible-frame-ref* to the front of the buffer.
3	For each LF in the buffer: If the noun represented by the LF is a possible frame reference, decide whether it should create a new MS or not (no new MS is needed if the noun refers to an element of an MS that is already present in the representation). If the LF is not marked as *possible-frame-ref*, determine which of the MSs in the database of the system contains the referent.
4	To answer the questions above, first order all MSs corresponding to a fixed-size preceding portion of the text using the heuristic function.
5	Compare the current LF with LFs of elements of known MSs. If the current LF represents a definite NP, try to find a direct match (a known element whose name is the same noun, a synonym or a hypernym) by examining several MSs (among those that received highest ranks in stage 4). If the current LF does not correspond to a definite NP, only the first MS in the ordering is considered.
6	Add the current LF to the chosen MS. Identify cases when a noun refers to a known element, an object in/part of a known bunch. The reference representation is updated using the following tags: OBJECT-CO-REF (coreference, the referent is an object) REFERS-TO-ALL (coreference, the referent is a bunch) POSSIBLE-ONE-OF-REF (the MS to which the current noun is added contains a *bunch* with the same name, and the current LF is marked as an *object*) POSSIBLE-PART-OF-REF (same as above, but the current LF is marked as a *bunch*)
7	Once MSs for all nouns of a sentence are known, a majority vote is taken and all LFs that did not receive one of the tags in stage 6 are reassigned to the MS that contains the highest number of nouns from this sentence. If a sentence contains a definite NP identified as an instance of coreference, the MS of its referent becomes the winner (no vote is taken)

Figure 4.1: A general description of the algorithm for nominal reference resolution.

A definite NP is likely to refer to an element that is already known. Therefore we examine several MSs from the ordering returned by the heuristic function. If the current LF and the LF of a known element have the same name and the same value of the bunch feature, we have identified an instance of coreference. If the current LF does not represent a definite NP, the algorithm can consider only the MS that received the highest rank from the heuristic function, because a noun with an indefinite or zero article can be referring to a new entity even if one of the known MSs already contains a bunch with the same name.

4.4 Analysis of Data from Modern English and Evaluation of Results

In order to test our system we ran it on a published English translation of an excerpt from *The Hunter Grachhus* (HG) by F. Kafka (1971:227–228). A manually annotated original of HG was presented in Chapter 3. We also tested our system on an excerpt from the first chapter of *Captain Blood* (CB) by R. Sabatini (1976:7–8). A referent is considered to be identified incorrectly when

1. a new entity was necessary, but an instance of coreference was reported;
2. a new entity was added when the actual referent was already present.

The results are as follows:

Table 4.1: Test results

Text	Number of NPs	Referent identified correctly	MS identified correctly
HG	100	99 (99%)	94 (94%)
CB	53	51 (96%)	50 (94%)
total	153	150 (98%)	144 (94%)

We shall show the output of our system (with the errors marked) run on HG after we discuss some short texts. Our first example contains two cases of coreference:

EXAMPLE 1

Sentences processed:

0 (YESTERDAY WE WENT TO A RESTAURANT)

1 (THE WAITER SAT US AT A TERRIBLE TABLE)
2 (AFTER DINNER WHEN THE WAITER SET OUR CHANGE DOWN ON THE TABLE HE IMMEDIATELY WALKED BACK OVER AND PICKED IT UP AGAIN)

Nouns:

0 (restaurant (NUMBER SG) (DEFINITE -) (BUNCH -) POSSIBLE-FRAME-REF)
1 (waiter (NUMBER SG) (DEFINITE +) (BUNCH -))
2 (table (NUMBER SG) (DEFINITE -) (BUNCH -))
3 (dinner (NUMBER SG) (DEFINITE ZERO) (BUNCH +))
4 (waiter (NUMBER SG) (DEFINITE +) (BUNCH -))
5 (change (NUMBER SG) (DEFINITE +) (BUNCH +))
6 (table (NUMBER SG) (DEFINITE +) (BUNCH -))

Mental spaces:

0 (MENT-SPACE NAME restaurant)
Elements:
<noun> <sentence number> <index in sentence> <index from beginning of text>

restaurant 0 0 0
waiter 1 0 1
OBJECT-CO-REF waiter 2 1 4
table 1 1 2
OBJECT-CO-REF table 2 3 6
dinner 2 0 3
change 2 2 5

In the following example we have two different referents with the same name. Both referring NPs are indefinite:

EXAMPLE 2

Sentences processed:

0 (YESTERDAY WE WENT TO A RESTAURANT)
1 (THE WAITER SAT US AT A TERRIBLE TABLE ALTHOUGH WE HAD BOOKED AN OUTSIDE TABLE IN ADVANCE)

Nouns:

0 (restaurant (NUMBER SG) (DEFINITE -) (BUNCH -)
POSSIBLE-FRAME-REF)
1 (waiter (NUMBER SG) (DEFINITE +) (BUNCH -))
2 (table (NUMBER SG) (DEFINITE -) (BUNCH -))
3 (table (NUMBER SG) (DEFINITE -) (BUNCH -))

Mental spaces:

0 (MENT-SPACE NAME restaurant)
Elements:
<noun> <sentence number> <index in sentence> <index from beginning of text>
restaurant 0 0 0
waiter 1 0 1
table 1 1 2
table 1 2 3

Our next several examples deal with objects in/parts of bunches:

EXAMPLE 3

Sentences processed:

0 (THERE WERE SEVERAL STUDENTS AND A PROFESSOR IN THE CLASSROOM)
1 (SOME STUDENTS WERE DISCUSSING THEIR WORK WITH THE PROFESSOR)

Nouns:

0 (student (NUMBER PL) (DEFINITE ZERO) (BUNCH +))
1 (professor (NUMBER SG) (DEFINITE -) (BUNCH -))

2 (classroom (NUMBER SG) (DEFINITE +) (BUNCH -)
POSSIBLE-FRAME-REF)
3 (student (NUMBER PL) (DEFINITE ZERO) (BUNCH +))
4 (work (NUMBER SG) (DEFINITE +) (BUNCH +))
5 (professor (NUMBER SG) (DEFINITE +) (BUNCH -))

Mental spaces:

0 (MENT-SPACE NAME classroom)
Elements:
<noun> <sentence number> <index in sentence> <index from beginning of text>
student 0 0 0
POSSIBLE-PART-OF-REF student 1 0 3
professor 0 1 1
OBJECT-CO-REF professor 1 2 5
classroom 0 2 2
student 1 0 3
work 1 1 4

EXAMPLE 4

Sentences processed:

0 (THERE WERE SEVERAL STUDENTS AND A PROFESSOR IN THE CLASSROOM)
1 (THE PROFESSOR WAS TALKING WITH A STUDENT)
2 (THAT STUDENT WAS VERY BRIGHT)

Nouns:

0 (student (NUMBER PL) (DEFINITE ZERO) (BUNCH +))
1 (professor (NUMBER SG) (DEFINITE -) (BUNCH -))
2 (classroom (NUMBER SG) (DEFINITE +) (BUNCH -) POSSIBLE-FRAME-REF)
3 (professor (NUMBER SG) (DEFINITE +) (BUNCH -))
4 (student (NUMBER SG) (DEFINITE -) (BUNCH -))
5 (student (NUMBER SG) (DEFINITE +) (BUNCH -))

Mental spaces:

0 (MENT-SPACE NAME classroom)
Elements:
<noun> <sentence number> <index in sentence> <index from beginning of text>
student 0 0 0
POSSIBLE-ONE-OF-REF student 1 1 4

professor 0 1 1
OBJECT-CO-REF professor 1 0 3
classroom 0 2 2
student 1 1 4
OBJECT-CO-REF student 2 0 5

EXAMPLE 5

Sentences processed:

0 (THERE WAS A LOT OF CHEESE IN THE KITCHEN)
1 (JAN WENT TO THE KITCHEN AND ATE SOME CHEESE)

Nouns:

0 (cheese (NUMBER SG) (DEFINITE ZERO) (BUNCH +))
1 (kitchen (NUMBER SG) (DEFINITE +) (BUNCH -) POSSIBLE-FRAME-REF)
2 (jan (NUMBER SG) (DEFINITE +) (BUNCH -))
3 (kitchen (NUMBER SG) (DEFINITE +) (BUNCH -) POSSIBLE-FRAME-REF)
4 (cheese (NUMBER SG) (DEFINITE ZERO) (BUNCH +))

Mental spaces:

0 (MENT-SPACE NAME kitchen)
Elements:
<noun> <sentence number> <index in sentence> <index from beginning of text>
cheese 0 0 0
POSSIBLE-PART-OF-REF cheese 1 2 4
kitchen 0 1 1
OBJECT-CO-REF kitchen 1 1 3
jan 1 0 2
cheese 1 2 4

In Example 5 we had two nouns marked as *possible-frame-ref*, yet only one MS was created.

EXAMPLE 6

Sentences processed:

0 (THERE WAS SOME CHEESE IN THE KITCHEN AND JAN ATE IT)
1 (BUT THE CHEESE WAS NOT MEANT TO BE BLUE AND IT WAS OFF)

Nouns:

0 (cheese (NUMBER SG) (DEFINITE ZERO) (BUNCH +))
1 (kitchen (NUMBER SG) (DEFINITE +) (BUNCH -) POSSIBLE-FRAME-REF)
2 (jan (NUMBER SG) (DEFINITE +) (BUNCH -))
3 (cheese (NUMBER SG) (DEFINITE +) (BUNCH +))

Mental spaces:

0 (MENT-SPACE NAME kitchen)
Elements:
<noun> <sentence number> <index in sentence> <index from beginning of text>
cheese 0 0 0
REFERS-TO-ALL cheese 1 0 3
kitchen 0 1 1
jan 0 2 2

A possible source of confusion for our system would be referring to a known object using a non-definite NP. Fortunately, this scenario does not seem to be frequent. The rest of this section shows the output of our program run on the fragment from *The Hunter Grachhus* with the errors marked.

Sentences processed:

0 (TWO BOYS WERE SITTING ON THE HARBOR WALL PLAYING WITH DICE)
1 (A MAN WAS READING A NEWSPAPER ON THE STEPS OF THE MONUMENT RESTING IN THE SHADOW OF A HERO WHO WAS FLOURISHING HIS SWORD ON HIGH)
2 (A GIRL WAS FILLING HER BUCKET AT THE FOUNTAIN)

3 (A FRUIT-SELLER WAS LYING BESIDE HIS WARES GAZING AT THE LAKE)
4 (THROUGH THE VACANT WINDOW AND DOOR OPENINGS OF A CAFE ONE COULD SEE TWO MEN QUITE AT THE BACK DRINKING THEIR WINE)
5 (THE PROPRIETOR WAS SITTING AT A TABLE IN FRONT AND DOZING)
6 (A BARK WAS SILENTLY MAKING FOR THE LITTLE HARBOR AS IF BORNE BY INVISIBLE MEANS OVER THE WATER)
7 (A MAN IN A BLUE BLOUSE CLIMBED ASHORE AND DREW THE ROPE THROUGH A RING)
8 (BEHIND THE BOATMAN TWO OTHER MEN IN DARK COATS WITH SILVER BUTTONS CARRIED A BIER ON WHICH BENEATH A GREAT FLOWER-PATTERNED FRINGED SILK CLOTH A MAN WAS APPARENTLY LYING)
9 (NOBODY ON THE QUAY TROUBLED ABOUT THE NEWCOMERS)
10 (EVEN WHEN THEY LOWERED THE BIER TO WAIT FOR THE BOATMAN WHO WAS STILL OCCUPIED WITH HIS ROPE NOBODY WENT NEARER NOBODY ASKED THEM A QUESTION NOBODY ACCORDED THEM AN INQUISITIVE GLANCE)
11 (THE PILOT WAS STILL FURTHER DETAINED BY A WOMAN WHO NOW APPEARED WITH LOOSENED HAIR ON THE DECK OF THE BOAT)
12 (THEN HE ADVANCED AND INDICATED A YELLOWISH TWO-STOREYED HOUSE THAT ROSE ABRUPTLY ON THE LEFT NEAR THE SEA)
13 (THE BEARERS TOOK UP THEIR BURDEN AND BORE IT TO THE LOW BUT GRACEFULLY PILLARED DOOR)
14 (A LITTLE BOY OPENED A WINDOW JUST IN TIME TO SEE THE PARTY VANISHING INTO THE HOUSE)
15 (THEN HE SHUT THE WINDOW AGAIN)
16 (THE DOOR TOO WAS NOW SHUT)
17 (A FLOCK OF DOVES WHICH HAD BEEN FLYING AROUND THE BELFRY ALIGHTED BEFORE THE HOUSE)
18 (AS IF THEIR FOOD WERE STORED WITHIN THEY ASSEMBLED IN FRONT OF THE DOOR)
19 (ONE OF THEM FLEW UP TO THE FIRST STORY AND PECKED AT THE WINDOWPANE)
20 (THEY WERE BRIGHT-HUED WELL-TENDED BEAUTIFUL BIRDS)

21 (THE WOMAN ON THE BOAT FLUNG GRAIN TO THEM IN A WIDE SWEEP)
22 (THEY ATE IT UP AND FLEW ACROSS TO THE WOMAN)
23 (A MAN IN A TOP HAT NOW DESCENDED ONE OF THE NARROW AND VERY STEEP LANES THAT LED TO THE HARBOR)
24 (HE GLANCED AROUND VIGILANTLY EVERYTHING SEEMED TO DISTRESS HIM)
25 (FRUIT SKINS WERE LYING ON THE STEPS OF THE MONUMENT HE SWEPT THEM OFF IN PASSING WITH HIS STICK)
26 (HE RAPPED AT THE HOUSE DOOR AT THE SAME TIME TAKING HIS TOP HAT FROM HIS HEAD WITH HIS BLACK-GLOVED HAND)
27 (THE DOOR WAS OPENED AT ONCE AND SOME FIFTY LITTLE BOYS APPEARED IN TWO ROWS IN THE LONG ENTRY HALL AND BOWED TO HIM)

Nouns:

0 (boy (NUMBER PL) (DEFINITE ZERO) (BUNCH +))
1 (harbor (NUMBER SG) (BUNCH -) POSSIBLE-FRAME-REF (FRAME-ADD (sea)))
2 (wall (NUMBER SG) (DEFINITE +) (BUNCH -))
3 (die (NUMBER PL) (DEFINITE ZERO) (BUNCH +))
4 (man (NUMBER SG) (DEFINITE -) (BUNCH -))
5 (newspaper (NUMBER SG) (DEFINITE -) (BUNCH -))
6 (step (NUMBER PL) (DEFINITE +) (BUNCH +))
7 (monument (NUMBER SG) (DEFINITE +) (BUNCH -) POSSIBLE-FRAME-REF)
8 (shadow (NUMBER SG) (DEFINITE +) (BUNCH -))
9 (hero (NUMBER SG) (DEFINITE -) (BUNCH -))
10 (sword (NUMBER SG) (DEFINITE +) (BUNCH -))
11 (girl (NUMBER SG) (DEFINITE -) (BUNCH -))
12 (bucket (NUMBER SG) (DEFINITE +) (BUNCH -))
13 (fountain (NUMBER SG) (DEFINITE +) (BUNCH -))
14 (fruit-seller (NUMBER SG) (DEFINITE -) (BUNCH -))
15 (ware (NUMBER PL) (DEFINITE +) (BUNCH +))
16 (lake (NUMBER SG) (DEFINITE +) (BUNCH -))
17 (window (NUMBER SG) (DEFINITE +) (BUNCH -))
18 (door (NUMBER SG) (BUNCH -))
19 (opening (NUMBER PL) (DEFINITE ZERO) (BUNCH +))

20 (cafe (NUMBER SG) (DEFINITE -) (BUNCH -)
POSSIBLE-FRAME-REF (FRAME-ADD (restaurant)))
21 (man (NUMBER PL) (DEFINITE ZERO) (BUNCH +))
22 (back (NUMBER SG) (DEFINITE +) (BUNCH -))
23 (wine (NUMBER SG) (DEFINITE +) (BUNCH +))
24 (proprietor (NUMBER SG) (DEFINITE +) (BUNCH -))
25 (table (NUMBER SG) (DEFINITE -) (BUNCH -))
26 (bark (NUMBER SG) (DEFINITE -) (BUNCH -) (HYPERNYMS
(ship)) POSSIBLE-FRAME-REF (FRAME-ADD (ship)))
27 (harbor (NUMBER SG) (DEFINITE +) (BUNCH -)
POSSIBLE-FRAME-REF (FRAME-ADD (sea)))
28 (mean (NUMBER PL) (DEFINITE ZERO) (BUNCH +))
29 (water (NUMBER SG) (DEFINITE +) (BUNCH +))
30 (man (NUMBER SG) (DEFINITE -) (BUNCH -))
31 (blouse (NUMBER SG) (DEFINITE -) (BUNCH -))
32 (rope (NUMBER SG) (DEFINITE +) (BUNCH -))
33 (ring (NUMBER SG) (DEFINITE -) (BUNCH -))
34 (boatman (NUMBER SG) (DEFINITE +) (BUNCH -) (HYPERNYMS
(man)) POSSIBLE-FRAME-REF (FRAME-ADD (ship)))
35 (man (NUMBER PL) (DEFINITE ZERO) (BUNCH +))
36 (coat (NUMBER PL) (DEFINITE ZERO) (BUNCH +))
37 (button (NUMBER PL) (DEFINITE ZERO) (BUNCH +))
38 (bier (NUMBER SG) (DEFINITE -) (BUNCH -))
39 (silk (NUMBER SG) (BUNCH +))
40 (cloth (NUMBER SG) (DEFINITE -) (BUNCH -))
41 (man (NUMBER SG) (DEFINITE -) (BUNCH -))
42 (quay (NUMBER SG) (DEFINITE +) (BUNCH -) (SYNONYMS
(wharf)))
43 (newcomer (NUMBER PL) (DEFINITE +) (BUNCH +))
44 (bier (NUMBER SG) (DEFINITE +) (BUNCH -))
45 (boatman (NUMBER SG) (DEFINITE +) (BUNCH -) (HYPERNYMS
(man)) POSSIBLE-FRAME-REF (FRAME-ADD (ship)))
46 (rope (NUMBER SG) (DEFINITE +) (BUNCH -))
47 (question (NUMBER SG) (DEFINITE -) (BUNCH -))
48 (glance (NUMBER SG) (DEFINITE -) (BUNCH -))
49 (pilot (NUMBER SG) (DEFINITE +) (BUNCH -))
50 (woman (NUMBER SG) (DEFINITE -) (BUNCH -))
51 (hair (NUMBER SG) (DEFINITE ZERO) (BUNCH +))
52 (deck (NUMBER SG) (DEFINITE +) (BUNCH -))

53 (boat (NUMBER SG) (DEFINITE +) (BUNCH -) (HYPERNYMS (ship)) POSSIBLE-FRAME-REF (FRAME-ADD (ship)))
54 (house (NUMBER SG) (DEFINITE -) (BUNCH -) POSSIBLE-FRAME-REF)
55 (sea (NUMBER SG) (DEFINITE +) (BUNCH -))
56 (bearer (NUMBER PL) (DEFINITE +) (BUNCH +))
57 (burden (NUMBER SG) (DEFINITE +) (BUNCH -))
58 (door (NUMBER SG) (DEFINITE +) (BUNCH -))
59 (boy (NUMBER SG) (DEFINITE -) (BUNCH -))
60 (window (NUMBER SG) (DEFINITE -) (BUNCH -))
61 (party (NUMBER SG) (DEFINITE +) (BUNCH -))
62 (house (NUMBER SG) (DEFINITE +) (BUNCH -) POSSIBLE-FRAME-REF)
63 (window (NUMBER SG) (DEFINITE +) (BUNCH -))
64 (door (NUMBER SG) (DEFINITE +) (BUNCH -))
65 (flock (NUMBER SG) (DEFINITE -) (BUNCH -))
66 (dove (NUMBER PL) (DEFINITE ZERO) (BUNCH +))
67 (belfry (NUMBER SG) (DEFINITE +) (BUNCH -))
68 (house (NUMBER SG) (DEFINITE +) (BUNCH -) POSSIBLE-FRAME-REF)
69 (food (NUMBER SG) (DEFINITE +) (BUNCH +))
70 (door (NUMBER SG) (DEFINITE +) (BUNCH -))
71 (story (NUMBER SG) (DEFINITE +) (BUNCH -))
72 (windowpane (NUMBER SG) (DEFINITE +) (BUNCH -))
73 (bird (NUMBER PL) (DEFINITE ZERO) (BUNCH +))
74 (woman (NUMBER SG) (DEFINITE +) (BUNCH -))
75 (boat (NUMBER SG) (DEFINITE +) (BUNCH -) (HYPERNYMS (ship)) POSSIBLE-FRAME-REF (FRAME-ADD (ship)))
76 (grain (NUMBER SG) (DEFINITE ZERO) (BUNCH +))
77 (sweep (NUMBER SG) (DEFINITE -) (BUNCH -))
78 (woman (NUMBER SG) (DEFINITE +) (BUNCH -))
79 (man (NUMBER SG) (DEFINITE -) (BUNCH -))
80 (top (NUMBER SG) (BUNCH -))
81 (hat (NUMBER SG) (DEFINITE -) (BUNCH -))
82 (lane (NUMBER PL) (DEFINITE +) (BUNCH +))
83 (harbor (NUMBER SG) (DEFINITE +) (BUNCH -) POSSIBLE-FRAME-REF (FRAME-ADD (sea)))
84 (fruit (NUMBER SG) (BUNCH +))
85 (skin (NUMBER PL) (DEFINITE ZERO) (BUNCH +))
86 (step (NUMBER PL) (DEFINITE +) (BUNCH +))

87 (monument (NUMBER SG) (DEFINITE +) (BUNCH -)
POSSIBLE-FRAME-REF)
88 (stick (NUMBER SG) (DEFINITE +) (BUNCH -))
89 (head (NUMBER SG) (DEFINITE +) (BUNCH -))
90 (house (NUMBER SG) (BUNCH -) POSSIBLE-FRAME-REF)
91 (door (NUMBER SG) (DEFINITE +) (BUNCH -))
92 (time (NUMBER SG) (DEFINITE +) (BUNCH +))
93 (top (NUMBER SG) (BUNCH -))
94 (hat (NUMBER SG) (DEFINITE +) (BUNCH -))
95 (hand (NUMBER SG) (DEFINITE +) (BUNCH -))
96 (door (NUMBER SG) (DEFINITE +) (BUNCH -))
97 (boy (NUMBER PL) (DEFINITE ZERO) (BUNCH +))
98 (row (NUMBER PL) (DEFINITE ZERO) (BUNCH +))
99 (entry (NUMBER SG) (BUNCH -))
100 (hall (NUMBER SG) (DEFINITE +) (BUNCH -))

Mental spaces:

0 (MENT-SPACE NAME harbor)
Elements:
<noun> <sentence number> <index in sentence> <index from beginning of text>
boy 0 0 0
harbor 0 1 1
OBJECT-CO-REF harbor 6 1 27
OBJECT-CO-REF harbor 23 4 83
wall 0 2 2
die 0 3 3
monument 1 3 7
girl 2 0 11
bucket 2 1 12
fruit-seller 3 0 14
ware 3 1 15
lake 3 2 16
back 4 5 22 error: wrong MS
table 5 1 25 error: wrong MS
bark 6 0 26
mean 6 2 28
water 6 3 29
man 7 0 30

OBJECT-CO-REF boatman 8 0 34
OBJECT-CO-REF boatman 10 1 45
blouse 7 1 31
ring 7 3 33
man 8 1 35
coat 8 2 36
button 8 3 37
bier 8 4 38
OBJECT-CO-REF bier 10 0 44
silk 8 5 39
cloth 8 6 40
man 8 7 41
question 10 3 47
glance 10 4 48
house 12 0 54
sea 12 1 55
windowpane 19 1 72 error: wrong MS
man 23 0 79
hat 23 2 81
OBJECT-CO-REF hat 26 5 94
lane 23 3 82

1 (MENT-SPACE NAME monument)
Elements:
<noun> <sentence number> <index in sentence> <index from beginning of text>
man 1 0 4
newspaper 1 1 5
step 1 2 6
REFERS-TO-ALL step 25 2 86
monument 1 3 7
OBJECT-CO-REF monument 25 3 87
shadow 1 4 8
hero 1 5 9
sword 1 6 10
fountain 2 2 13
cafe 4 3 20 error: wrong MS
newcomer 9 1 43 error: wrong MS
party 14 2 61 error: wrong MS
fruit 25 0 84

skin 25 1 85
stick 25 4 88

2 (MENT-SPACE NAME cafe)
Elements:
<noun> <sentence number> <index in sentence> <index from beginning of text>
window 4 0 17
door 4 1 18
opening 4 2 19
cafe 4 3 20
man 4 4 21
wine 4 6 23
proprietor 5 0 24

3 (MENT-SPACE NAME bark)
Elements:
<noun> <sentence number> <index in sentence> <index from beginning of text>
bark 6 0 26
OBJECT-CO-REF boat 11 4 53
OBJECT-CO-REF boat 21 1 75
rope 7 2 32
OBJECT-CO-REF rope 10 2 46
quay 9 0 42
pilot 11 0 49 error: wrong REF
woman 11 1 50
OBJECT-CO-REF woman 21 0 74
OBJECT-CO-REF woman 22 0 78
hair 11 2 51
deck 11 3 52
bearer 13 0 56
burden 13 1 57
grain 21 2 76
sweep 21 3 77

4 (MENT-SPACE NAME house)
Elements:
<noun> <sentence number> <index in sentence> <index from beginning of text>
house 12 0 54

OBJECT-CO-REF house 14 3 62
OBJECT-CO-REF house 17 3 68
ADJ-CO-REF house 26 1 90
door 13 2 58
OBJECT-CO-REF door 16 0 64
OBJECT-CO-REF door 18 1 70
OBJECT-CO-REF door 26 2 91
OBJECT-CO-REF door 27 0 96
boy 14 0 59
window 14 1 60
OBJECT-CO-REF window 15 0 63
flock 17 0 65
dove 17 1 66
belfry 17 2 67
food 18 0 69
story 19 0 71
bird 20 0 73
head 26 0 89
time 26 3 92
hand 26 6 95
boy 27 1 97
row 27 2 98
entry 27 3 99
hall 27 4 100

• CHAPTER FIVE •

Application of the Proposed Approach to Data from Earlier Periods of the German Language

5.1 Old High German

In this section we discuss the use of articles in OHG text fragments from Tatian and Notker. The OHG simple demonstrative pronoun *dër (thër)* had the following forms (Braune 1987:243):

		masc.		neut.	fem.
sg.	nom.	*dër*		*daz*	*diu*
	gen.		*dës*		*dëra, (dëru, -o)*
	dat.		*dëmu, dëmo*		*dëru, -o*
	acc.	*dën*		*daz*	*dea, dia, (die)*
	instr.		*diu*		
pl.	nom., acc.	*de, dea, dia, die*		*diu, (dei)*	*deo, dio*
	gen.			*dëro*	
	dat.			*dem, den, (deam, dien)*	

Dër served not only as a demonstrative pronoun, but also as a relative pronoun, and as a definite article. Hodler (1954:9) calls *dër* used to ex-pressed definiteness (Bestimmtheit) only—and not as a demonstrative pronoun—a "rein realisierender Artikel". Such cases are quite common already in Tatian (written around 830 A.D.), as well as in Notker, whose work dates from a later period (around 1000 A.D.). For each fragment we give its full OHG original with English glosses, followed by analysis of the articles that occur in the text.

Tatian (Sievers 1892:47–49, 287–289)

22
7. Inti giengun tho zi imo sine iungiron,
And came up to him his disciples,
inti úfarhabanen sinen ougon in sie
and [he] raised his eyes at them
íntteta sinan mund, lérta sie sús quedanti:
opened his mouth, taught them so saying:
8. Salige sint thie thar arme sint in geiste,
Blessed are those who are poor in ZERO-ART spirit,
uuanta thero ist gotes rihhi.
for theirs is ZERO-ART God's kingdom.
9. Salige sint manduuare,
Blessed are meek [people],
uuanta thie bisizzent erda.
for they own ZERO-ART earth.
10. Salige sint thie thar vvuofent, uuanta thie uuerdent gifluobrit.
Blessed are those who mourn, for they will be comforted.
11. Salige sint thie thar
Blessed are those who
hungerent inti thurstent reht,
hunger and thirst for ZERO-ART righteousness,
uuanta thie uuerdent gisatote.
for they will be filled.
12. Salige sint thie thar sint miltherze,
Blessed are those who are merciful,
uuanta sie folgent miltidun.
for they follow ZERO-ART mercy.
13. Salige sint thie thar sint subere in herzon,
Blessed are those who are pure in ZERO-ART heart,
uuanta thie gisehent got.
for they will see ZERO-ART God
14. Salige sint thie thar sint sibbisame,
Blessed are those who are peacemakers,
uuanta sie gotes barn sint ginemnit.
for they ZERO-ART God's suns are called.
15. Salige sint thie thar ahtnessi sint tholenti
Blessed are those who are persecuted

thuruh reht,
because of ZERO-ART righteousness,
uuanta iro ist himilo rihhi.
for theirs is ZERO-ART heavens' kingdom.
16. Salige birut ír, mit thiu iu fluohhont inti hazzont iuúih man
Blessed are you, when curse and hate you people,
inti ahtent iuúar inti quedent ál ubil uuidar íu liogente,
and persecute you and say all evil against you falsely,
mit thiu sie iuuih ziskeident inti itiuuizzont
when they you separate and mock
inti áruuerphent iuuaran namon samasó ubil
and decry your name as evil
thuruh then mannes sún.
through DEF-ART Son of Man.
17. Giuehet in themo tage inti blidet,
Rejoice on that day and be glad,
uuanta bithiu iuuar mieta ist ginuhtsam
for your reward is great
in himilon.
in ZERO-ART heavens.
18. Só áhtitun sie thero uuizagono
In the same way persecuted they DEF-ART prophets
thie thar fora íu uuarun, iro fatera.
who before you were, their fathers.

23
1. Thoh uuidaro uúe iu otagon,
But woe to you [who are] rich,
uuanta ir habet íuuuera fluobara.
for you have your comfort.
2. Uue íu thie thar gisatote birut,
Woe to you who fed are,
bithiu uuanta ír hungeret.
for you will be hungry.
3. Uue íu thie nú lahhet,
Woe to you who now laugh,
bithiu uuanta ír vvuofet inti riozet.
for you will mourn and weep.
4. Uue íu mit thiu íu uuolaquœdent alle man:
Woe to you when of you speak well all men,

after thesen tatun luggen uuizagon iro fatera.
that is how treated ZERO-ART false prophets their fathers.

24
1. Uzouh iu thie dar gihoret, quidu ih:
But to you who listen, say I:
ír birut salz erda.
you are ZERO-ART salt of ZERO-ART earth.
2. Oba thaz salz áritalet,
But if DEF-ART salt loses its saltiness,
in hiu selzit man iz thanne?
how makes salty one it then?
3. Zi niouuihtu mag íz elihor, nibi thaz man íz úzuuerphe,
For nothing can it be useful, except to be thrown out
inti si fúrtretan fon mannun.
and trampled by ZERO-ART men.

241
1. Einlif iungoron giengun in Galileam
ZERO-ART eleven disciples went to Galilee
in then berg thar ín ther heilant gimarcota,
to DEF-ART mountain which to them DEF-ART Savior indicated,
inti gisehenti inan betotun ínan,
and when they saw him, [they] worshiped him,
sume giuuesso zuuehotun.
some doubted.
2. Inti ituuizzota iro ungiloubfulli
And [he] rebuked them for their lack of faith
inti thia hertida thes hérzen,
and DEF-ART callousness of DEF-ART heart,
uuanta then thie ínan gisahun erstantan ni giloubtun.
because [they] those who him saw resurrected did not believe.

242
1. Inti sprah ín zuo quędenti:
And spoke to them saying:
gigeban ist al giuualt mir
given is all authority to me
in himile inti in erdu.
in ZERO-ART heaven and on ZERO-ART earth.

2. Gét in alla uueralt, praedigot euangelium
go in all world, preach ZERO-ART gospel
allera giscéfti inti leret alle thíota,
to all creation and teach all nations,
toufenti sie in namen
baptizing them in ZERO-ART name
fater inti súnes inti
of ZERO-ART Father and ZERO-ART Son and
thes heilagen geistes;
DEF-ART Holy Spirit;
leret sie zi bihaltanne alliu so uúelichiu so ih íu gibot.
teach them to obey everything as I you commanded.
3. Inti senu ih bin mit íu allen tagon
And see I am with you all days
unzan enti uúeralti.
until ZERO-ART end of ZERO-ART world.

As we can see, in the fragment above the zero article often occurs in cases where in Modern German the definite article would be used:

(22.8 r) Salige sint thie thar arme sint in geiste...
Blessed are those who are poor in ZERO-ART spirit

(22.9 r) Salige sint manduuare,
Blessed are meek [people],
uuanta thie bisizzent erda.
for they own ZERO-ART earth.

(22.13 r) Salige sint thie thar sint subere in herzon...
Blessed are those who are pure in ZERO-ART heart

(24.1 r) ír birut salz erda
you are ZERO-ART salt of ZERO-ART earth

(242.2 r) inti leret alle thíota,
and teach all nations,
toufenti sie in namen
baptizing them in ZERO-ART name
fater inti súnes
of ZERO-ART Father and ZERO-ART Son

inti thes heilagen geistes...
and DEF-ART Holy Spirit...

(242.3 r) ih bin mit íu allen tagon
I am with you all days
unzan enti uúeralti.
until ZERO-ART end of ZERO-ART world.

In cases where the definite article is used, the referent possesses all characteristics required by Rules 1 and 5:

(22.16 r) mit thiu sie iuuih ziskeident inti itiuuizzont
when they you separate and mock
inti áruuerphent iuuaran namon samasó ubil
and decry your name as evil
thuruh then mannes sún.
through DEF-ART Son of Man.
[s World, r 1]

(241.1 r) Einlif iungoron giengun in Galileam
ZERO-ART eleven disciples went to Galilee
in then berg thar
to DEF-ART mountain which
[s Galilee, r 1]
ín ther heilant gimarcota...
to them DEF-ART Savior indicated
[s World, r 1]

(242.2) toufenti sie in namen
baptizing them in ZERO-ART name
fater inti súnes
of ZERO-ART Father and ZERO-ART Son
inti thes heilagen geistes;
and DEF-ART Holy Spirit;
[s World, r 1]

If we use Gundel's terminology, a demonstrative pronoun requires a higher degree of definiteness than the definite article. The fact that in OHG the article is relatively young suggests that its uses should be mostly restricted to the segment of the Givenness Hierarchy that corresponds to demonstrative pronouns. For instance, in the following fragment the status

ACTIVATED of *thaz salz* 'DEF-ART salt' is due to an explicit introduction of the referent:

(24.1–2 r) ír birut salz erda
you are ZERO-ART salt of ZERO-ART earth.
Oba thaz salz áritalet...
But if DEF-ART salt loses its saltiness
[s World, r 5]

Yet we also find cases where the definite article is used with a noun whose referent is an element of a frame that was *not* directly mentioned before:

(241.2 r) Inti ituuizzota iro ungiloubfulli
And rebuked [them for] their lack of faith
inti thia hertida thes hérzen,
and DEF-ART callousness of DEF-ART heart,
[s Heart, r 1] [s Human, r 1]
uuanta then thie ínan gisahun erstantan ni giloubtun.
because [they] those who him saw resurrected did not believe.

The status of both *thia hertida* 'DEF-ART callousness' and *thes hérzen* 'of DEF-ART heart' is UNIQUELY IDENTIFIABLE; such cases are closer to the modern use of the definite article because here its role is to mark definiteness and not anaphora or deixis alone.

Notker (1983: 510–512)

Psalm 138

7. Quo ibo a spiritu tuo?
Where can I go from your Spirit?
Vuára mag ih fore dînemo geîste
Where can I [go] from your Spirit,
des diu uuerlt fol íst?
of which DEF-ART world full is?
Also iz chit: Spiritus domini repleuit orbem terrarum.
It is also said: The Spirit of the Lord fills the whole world.
Et quo a facie tua fugiam? Unde uuára fliêho ih fóre dír?
Where can I flee from your presence? And where flee I from you?
Uuara mag ih indrínnen dînero abolgi?
Where can I escape from your wrath?

8. Si ascendero in caelum, tu illic es: Héue ih mih hóho,
If I go up to the heavens, you are there: If I go up high,
dâr drúcchest du mih uuídere. Si in infernum descendero, ades:
there push you me back. If (I) descend to Hell, you are there:
Pirgo ih mih, daz ih mînero sundon iéhen neuuíle,
If hide I myself, so that I my sins do not admit,
dû geiíhtest mih íro.
you make me admit them.

9. Si recipiam pennas meas in directum
If I take the wings of the morning
et habitabo in extrema maris (id est seculi):
and dwell in the uttermost parts of the sea (that is of the world)
Ube ih mîne féttacha (daz chit: amorem dei et proximi)
If I my wings (that means: love for God and neighbor)
ze mir nímo in geríhti unde ih púuuo
to me took in righteousness and I lived
daz chit: râmen mit kedingi
that means: hoping to stay
ze ende dírro uuérlte,
until ZERO-ART end of DEF-ART world
so dies iudicii ist,
as this the Judgment Day is,
uuanda dar ist ende dísses uuerltméres,
for there is ZERO-ART end of this world sea,
ze déro uuîs indrinno ih dînero abolgi.
(If) in this way escaped I from your wrath,

10. Etenim illuc manus tua deducet me
even there your hand shall lead me,
et tenebit me dextera tua:
and your right hand shall hold me:
Dára ze demo ende bringet mih dîn hant
Event to that end would bring me your hand
unde dîn zeseuua habet mih,
and your right hand would protect me,
daz ih ín den mére nesturze,
so that I into DEF-ART sea do not fall,
êr ih ín uberfliege.
before I over it fly.

11. Et dixi: fortasse tenebrae conculcabunt me:
And I said: surely the darkness shall cover me:
Unde chad ih fórhtendo:
And said I in fear:
ódeuuâno fînisterîna trêttônt mih
surely ZERO-ART darkness shall cover me
unde írrent mih. Uuaz sint die finstri ane díser lîb?
and derange me. What is DEF-ART darkness other than this life?
Et nox illuminatio in deliciis meis:
The night has become light to my joy:
Unde bedíu ist min naht, daz chit: min lîb
And therefore has my night, that is: my life
lîeht uuorden an minero lússami,
ZERO-ART light become to my joy,
daz ist: Christus. Er chám in disa naht, daz er sie irlîehti.
that is: Christ. He came in this night, so that he it illuminates.

12. Quia tenebrae non tenebrantur a te:
even the darkness is not dark to you
Uuanda fón dir, Christe,
for because of you, Christ,
nefinstrent die finstri,
does not become dark DEF-ART darkness,
nube fone démo, der sîne sunda
but because of the one, who his sins
bírget unde iro neiiehet.
hides and them does not admit.
Der zuífaltôt diê finstri.
He magnifies DEF-ART darkness.
Et nox tamquam dies illuminabitur:
And the night is bright as the day:
Unde rehtemo man uuirt
And for ZERO-ART righteous man becomes
diu naht sámo lîehte so der tag,
DEF-ART night as bright as DEF-ART day
daz chit: aduersitas netárot imo nieht
this means: misfortunes happen to him not
mêr danne prosperitas.
more than good luck.

Sicut tenebrae eius ita et lumen eius:
darkness is as light with him
Imo gant prospera unde aduersa gelicho.
For him good luck and bad luck are the same.

13. Quia tu possedisti renes meos, domine:
For you possess my inward parts, Lord:
Uuanda dû habest pesézzen, mîne láncha,
For you possess my inward parts
du nehengest mir únchíusce gelúste.
you do not allow me ZERO-ART evil wishes.
Suscepisti me ex utero matris meae:
You took me from my mothers womb
Dû habest mih kenómen uzer mînero muoter uuombo.
You have me taken from my mother's womb.
Daz ist díu zâliga Babylonia,
This is DEF-ART horrible Babel,
dero chint Ierusalem caelestem neminnont.
whose children Heavenly Jerusalem do not like.

14. Confitebor tibi, domine,
I want to confess to you, Lord
quoniam terribiliter mirificatus es:
that you fearfully wonderful are:
Ih iîeho dir, tróhten,
I confess to you, Lord,
daz du egebâro uns uuunderlih uuorden bist
that you fearfully to us wonderful have become
Mira opera tua, deus, et anima mea cognoscet nimis:
Wonderful are your works, Lord, my soul knows them well.
Daz ist one díu, uuanda diniu uuerch uuunderlih sint,
This is because your works wonderful are,
gót, unde siu nu min sêla harto uuóla bechénnet,
God, and them now my soul very well knows,
souuio ih in fore nieht zuo nemahti.
as I them before did not understand.

15. Non est absconditum os meum, s. a te, quod fecisti in abscondito:
My frame was not hidden from you, you created it in secret
Dir ist únferbórgen min stárchi die du mir tâte tougeno.
For you is not hidden my strength which you to me gave in secret.

Fóne dero chad Paulus: Non solum autem sed
of which said Paul: Not only so, but
et gloriamur in tribulationibus.
we also rejoice in our sufferings,
Et substantia mea in inferioribus terrae, id est: in carne:
Also my substance in the depths of the earth, that is: in the flesh
Unde ist min sela in dero tiefi des lîchamen,
And is my soul in DEF-ART depth of DEF-ART flesh,
doh iro diu starchi gegében si.
yet to it DEF-ART strength given is.

Again, we see uses of the zero article where Modern German would require a definite article:

(9 r) daz chit: râmen mit kedingi ze ende
that means: hoping to stay until ZERO-ART end
dírro uuérlte...
of DEF-ART world

(9 r) uuanda dar ist ende dísses uuerltméres...
for there is ZERO-ART end of this world sea

The definite article occurs before nouns referring to objects that are unique in the world:

(7 r) Uuára mag ih fore dînemo geîste
Where can I [go] from your Spirit,
des diu uuerlt fol íst?
of which DEF-ART world full is?
[s World, r 1]

(9 r) daz chit: râmen mit kedingi ze ende
that means: hoping to stay until ZERO-ART end
dírro uuérlte...
of DEF-ART world
[s World, r 1]

(13 r) *Dû habest mih kenómen uzer mînero muoter uuombo.*
You have me taken from my mother's womb.

Daz ist díu zâliga Babylonia,
This is DEF-ART horrible Babel,
[s World, r 1]
dero chint Ierusalem caelestem neminnont.
whose children Heavenly Jerusalem do not like.

There are also cases where the status ACTIVATED, that warrants the use of the definite article, is a result of a previous explicit introduction of the referent:

(9 r) uuanda dar ist ende dísses uuerltméres...
for there is ZERO-ART end of this world sea...
dîn zeseuua habet mih,
your right hand would protect me,

(10 r) daz ih ín den mére nesturze...
so that I into DEF-ART sea do not fall
[s World, r 1]

(11 r) Unde chad ih fórhtendo:
And said I in fear:
ódeuuâno finisterîna trêttônt mih
surely ZERO-ART darkness shall cover me
unde írrent mih. Uuaz sint die finstri ane díser lîb?
and derange me. What is DEF-ART darkness but this life?
[s World, r 5]

(12 r) Quia tenebrae non tenebrantur a te:
even the darkness is not dark to you
Uuanda fón dir, Christe,
for because of you, Christ,
nefinstrent die finstri,
does not become dark DEF-ART darkness,
[s World, r 5]
nube fone démo, der sîne sunda
but because of the one, who his sins
bírget unde iro neiiehet.
hides and them does not admit.
Der zuífaltôt diê finstri.
He magnifies DEF-ART darkness.
[s World, r 5]

Finally, just as in the fragment from Tatian before, there are cases where the definite article is used with nouns whose referents are UNIQUELY IDENTIFIABLE. In the following example *naht* 'night' was mentioned before, but not *tag* 'day':

(11 r) *Unde bedíu ist min naht, daz chit: min lîb*
And therefore has my night, that is: my life
lîeht uuorden an minero lússami...
light become to my joy...
Unde rehtemo man uuirt
And for ZERO-ART righteous man becomes
diu naht sámo lîehte so der tag...
DEF-ART night as bright as DEF-ART day
[s Day, r 1] [s Day, r 1]

Similarly, in the next example only *starchi* 'strength' was mentioned before:

(15 r) Non est absconditum os meum, s. a te,
My frame was not hidden from you,
quod fecisti in abscondito:
you created it in secret
Dir ist únferbórgen min stárchi die du mir tâte tougeno.
For you is not hidden my strength which you to me gave in secret.
Unde ist min sela in dero tiefi des lîchamen,
And is my soul in DEF-ART depth of DEF-ART flesh,
[s Human Body, r 1] [s Human Body, r 1]
doh iro diu starchi gegében si.
yet to it DEF-ART strength given is.
[s Human Body, r 1]

5.2 Middle High German

The forms of the definite article in MHG are as follows (Paul 1959:145):

		masc.		neut.	fem.
sg.	nom.	*dër*		*daz*	*diu*
	gen.		*dës*		*dër(e)*
	dat.		*dëm(e)*		*dër(e)*
	acc.	*dën*		*daz*	*die*
pl.	nom., acc.	*die*		*diu*	*die*
	gen.			*dër(e)*	
	dat.			*dën*	

We analyze fragments from *Das Nibelungenlied* and *Tristan*. The use of articles in these texts is close to modern, so we indicate the mental space and the rule corresponding to a noun with an article in the usual way below the gloss line. After each fragment, we analyze the composition of mental spaces that it represents and their affect on the choice of articles.

Das Nibelungenlied (Bartsch 1870:77–79)

8. Aventiure
Adventure 8

482
Dannen gie dô Sîfrit
From there went then Siegfried
zer porten ûf den sant
to DEF-ART harbor on DEF-ART sand
[s Isenstein, r 1] [s Harbor, r 5]
in sîner tarnkappen
in his magic cloak
da er ein schiffel vant.
where he INDEF-ART boat found.
[s Harbor, r 2]
dar an sô stuont vil tougen
in it so stood hidden
daz Sigemundes kint:
DEF-ART Siegmund's son
[s World, r 1]

er fuort ez balde dannen,
he drove it soon from there,
alsam ez waete der wint.
as if was blowing DEF-ART wind.
[s Sea, r 1]

483
Den schefmeister sach niemen:
DEF-ART steersman saw none
[s Ship, r 1]
daz schiffel sêre vlôz
DEF-ART boat fast moved
[s Sea, r 1]
von Sîfrides kreften
by Siegfried's strengths
die wâren alsô grôz.
which were so great.
si wânden daz ez fuorte
they thought that it drove on
ein sunderstarker wint:
INDEF-ART unusually strong wind:
[s Sea, r 2]
nein, ez fuorte Sîfrit
no, it moved Siegfried
der schoenen Sigelinde kint
of DEF-ART beautiful Siegelind son
[s World, r 1]

484
Bî des tages zîte
in of DEF-ART day time
[s Day, r 1]
unt in der einen naht
and of one night
kom er zeinem lande
came he to INDEF-ART land
[s Sea, r 2]
mit groezlîcher maht
with ZERO-ART great power
[s Sea, r 6]

wol hundert langer raste
of full ZERO-ART hundred long rests
[s The Land of the Nibelungs, r 6]
unde dannoch paz:
and more than that:
die hiezen Nibelunge,
These [people] were Nibelungs,
dâ er den grôzen hort besaz.
there he DEF-ART great hoard owned.
[s The Land of the Nibelungs, r 1]

485
Der helt fuor aleine
DEF-ART hero drove alone
[s Sea, r 1]
ûf einen wert vil breit:
to INDEF-ART island very wide:
[s Sea, r 2]
daz shif gebant vil balde
DEF-ART boat tied soon
[s Harbor, r 1]
der ritter vil gemeit.
DEF-ART knight with great might.
[s Harbor, r 1]
er gie zeinem berge,
he went to INDEF-ART hill,
[s The Land of the Nibelungs, r 2]
dar ûf ein burc stuont
on which INDEF-ART castle stood
[s The Land of the Nibelungs, r 2]
unt suochte herberge,
and sought lodgment,
sô noch die wegemüeden tuont.
as still the way-worn [travelers] do.

486
Dô kom er für die porten:
Then came he to DEF-ART gate:
[s Castle, r 1]

verslozzen im diu stuont
closed for him which stood
ja huoten si ir êren,
and guarded they their honor,
sô noch die liute tuont
as still DEF-ART people do
[s World, r 5]
anz tor begunde bôzen
on DEF-ART door began to knock
[s Castle, r 1]
der unkunde man
DEF-ART stranger
[s Castle, r 1]
daz was vil wol behüetet:
which was very well guarded
dô vant er innerthalben stan
here found he within stood

487
Einen ungefüegen
INDEF-ART giant
[s Castle, r 2]
der der bürge pflac,
who DEF-ART castle kept
[s Castle, r 1]
bî dem zallen zîten
at whose side at all times
sîn gewaefen lac.
his arms lay.
der sprach wer ist der bôzet
he spoke who is it who is knocking
sô vaste an daz tor?
so rudely on DEF-ART gate?
[s Castle, r 1]
dô wandelt sîne stimme
then changed his voice
der küene Sîfrit dâ vor
DEF-ART bold Siegfried before it
[s Castle, r 1]

488
Er sprach ich pin ein recke
he spoke I am INDEF-ART knight
[s Castle, r 2]
entsliuz ûf daz tor.
open DEF-ART gate.
[s Castle, r 1]
ich erzürne ir eteslîchen
I will enrage you all
noch hiute dâ vor,
more today outside
der gerne sampfte laege
who would want to lie soft
unt hete sîn gemach.
and take his ease.
daz muot den portenaere
this irked DEF-ART warder
[s Castle, r 1]
dô daz Sîfrit gesprach
when this Siegfried spoke

489
Nu het der rise küene
Now had DEF-ART giant bold
[s Castle, r 1]
sîn gwaefen an getân,
his armor put on
sînen helm ûf sîn houbet
his helm upon his head
der vil starke man
DEF-ART very strong man
[s Castle, r 1]
den schilt er balde zuhte
DEF-ART shield he quickly picked up
[s Armor, r 1]
daz tor er ûf dô swief:
DEF-ART gate he opened wide:
[s Castle, r 1]
wi rehte gremelîchen
how indeed fiercely

er an Sîvriden lief !
he at Siegfried ran!

490
Wie er getorste wecken
how he dared to wake up
sô manigen küenen man.
so many valiant men.
dâ wurden slege swinde
then were ZERO-ART blows mighty
[s Castle, r 6]
von sîner hant getan.
by his hand dealt out.
dô begonde im schirmen
then began himself to defend
der hêrlîche gast
DEF-ART lordly guest
[s Castle, r 1]
dô scuof der portenaere
but achieved DEF-ART warder
[s Castle, r 1]
daz sîn gespenge zebrast
that his shield-plates fell apart

491
Von einer îsenstangen:
With INDEF-ART iron bar:
[s Armor, r 2]
des gie dem helde nôt.
was DEF-ART hero in need.
[s Castle, r 1]
ein teil begonde fürhten
at once began to fear
Sîfrit den tôt
Siegfried DEF-ART death
[s Life, r 1]
dô der portenaere
when DEF-ART warder
[s Castle, r 1]

sô krefteclîchen sluoc.
so strongly hit
dar umbe was im waege
therefore him liked
sîn herre Sîvrit genuoc.
his lord Siegfied a lot.

492
Si striten alsô sêre
they fought so fiercely
daz al diu burc erscal.
that all DEF-ART castle rang.
[s Castle, r 1]
dô hôrte man daz diezen
then heard one this noise
in Nibelunges sal.
in Nibelung's hall.
er twanc den portenaere,
he overcame DEF-ART warder
[s Castle, r 1]
daz er in sit gebant.
so that he him bound.
diu maere wurden künde
DEF-ART tale became known
[s Castle, r 1]
in al der Nibelunge lant
in all DEF-ART Nibelungs' land
[s The Land of the Nibelungs, r 5]

493
Dô hôrt daz grimme strîten
then heard DEF-ART fierce fighting
[s Castle, r 1]
verre durch den berc
far across DEF-ART hill
[s The Land of the Nibelungs, r 1]
Albrich der vil küene,
Alberich DEF-ART very bold,
[s The Land of the Nibelungs, r 1]

ein wildiz getwerc.
INDEF-ART savage dwarf.
[s The Land of the Nibelungs, r 2]
er wâfende sich balde
he armed himself quickly
dô lief er dâ er vant
and ran he where he found
disen gast vil edelen,
this guest very noble,
da er den starken gebant
as he DEF-ART strong man bound.
[s Castle, r 1]

The referents of most nouns in the fragment lie in one of four mental spaces: Harbor, Sea, The Land of the Nibelungs, and Castle. The spaces Harbor, Sea and Castle are instantiated frames.

The space Harbor is first introduced with the NP *zer porten* 'to DEF-ART harbor' where the definite article is due to the uniqueness of the object in the MS Isenstein. Harbor becomes the current MS; two elements of this MS are mentioned next: *den sant* 'DEF-ART sand' and *ein schiffel* 'INDEF-ART boat'. *Sant* with a definite article refers to an element viewed as part of the frame, while a representation for INDEF-ART *schiffel* is added to the MS as a new entity:

(482 r) Dannen gie dô Sîfrit
From there went then Siegfried
zer porten ûf den sant
to DEF-ART harbor on DEF-ART sand
[s Isenstein, r 1] [s Harbor, r 5]
in sîner tarnkappen
in his magic cloak
da er ein schiffel vant.
where he INDEF-ART boat found.
[s Harbor, r 2]

Siegfried leaves the harbor, and *Sea* becomes the MS for the next part of the poem. We see another reference to *schiffel* 'ship'—this time with a definite article, and a reference to an element of the frame Ship: *den schefmeister* 'DEF-ART steersman'. The latter is implicitly introduced by the frame:

(483 r) *Den schefmeister sach niemen:*
DEF-ART steersman saw none
[s Ship, r 1]
daz schiffel sêre vlôz
DEF-ART boat fast moved
[s Sea, r 1]

The journey ends when an island is reached. The corresponding NPs are *einem lande* 'INDEF-ART land' and *einen wert* 'INDEF-ART island'. There are also additional references to *der helt* 'DEF-ART hero' and *daz shif* 'DEF-ART boat', as expected, with the definite article:

(484 r) kom er zeinem lande
came he to INDEF-ART land
[s Sea, r 2]

(485 r) Der helt fuor aleine
DEF-ART hero drove alone
[s Sea, r 1]
ûf einen wert vil breit:
to INDEF-ART island very wide:
[s Sea, r 2]
daz shif gebant vil balde
DEF-ART boat tied soon
[s Harbor, r 1]

The next MS is The Land of the Nibelungs. Two new entities from this MS are introduced with an indefinite article: *einem berge* 'INDEF-ART hill' and *ein burc* 'INDEF-ART castle':

(485 r) er gie zeinem berge,
he went to INDEF-ART hill,
[s The Land of the Nibelungs, r 2]
dar ûf ein burc stuont
on which INDEF-ART castle stood
[s The Land of the Nibelungs, r 2]

The MS The Land of the Nibelungs is followed by Castle. The author refers to its gate with definite NPs: *die porten* 'DEF-ART gate', *anz tor* 'on DEF-ART door':

(486 r) Dô kom er für die porten
Then came he to DEF-ART gate
[s Castle, r 1]

(486 r) anz tor begunde bôzen
on DEF-ART door began to knock
[s Castle, r 1]
der unkunde man
DEF-ART stranger
[s Castle, r 1]

Then a new entity—*einen ungefüegen* 'INDEF-ART giant'—is added:

(487 r) dô vant er innerthalben stan
here found he within stood
Einen ungefüegen
INDEF-ART giant
[s Castle, r 2]
der der bürge pflac
who DEF-ART castle kept
[s Castle, r 1]

Subsequent references to the warder occur with the definite article: *den portenaere* 'DEF-ART warder', *der rise* 'DEF-ART giant' :

(488–489 r) daz muot den portenaere
this irked DEF-ART warder
[s Castle, r 1]
dô daz Sîfrit gesprach
when this Siegfried spoke
Nu het der rise küene
Now had DEF-ART giant bold
[s Castle, r 1]
sîn gwaefen an getân
his armor put on

A fight breaks out. First reference to it is made with a pl. noun with zero article: *slege* 'ZERO-ART blows', a definite NP referring to the fight itself follows: *daz grimme strîten* 'DEF-ART fierce fighting':

(490 r) dâ wurden slege swinde
then were ZERO-ART blows mighty
[s Castle, r 6]
von sîner hant getan.
by his hand dealt out.

(493 r) Dô hôrt daz grimme strîten
then heard DEF-ART fierce fighting
[s Castle, r 1]
verre durch den berc
far across DEF-ART hill
[s The Land of the Nibelungs, r 1]

Den berc 'DEF-ART hill' is an element of the MS The Land of the Nibelungs which was already mentioned in verse 485.

Tristan (Bechstein 1873:81–84)

Die Entführung
The Abduction

In den zîten unde dô
In those times and then

2150
kam ez von âventiure alsô,
came it to pass by chance
[the expression *von âventiure* 'by chance', also occurs below in verse 2215]
daz von Norwaege über sê
that from Norway across ZERO-ART sea
[idiomatic]
ein koufschif unde dekeinez mê
one trading ship, and no more
in daz lant ze Parmenîe kam
to DEF-ART country of Parmenie came
[s World, r 1]
und sîn gelende dâ genam
and its landfall there made

und ûz gestiez ze Canoêl
and put to shore at Canoel
vür daz selbe castêl,
at that same castle,
dâ der marschalc ze staete
where DEF-ART marshal always
[s Parmenie, r 1]
sîn wesen ûfe haete
his residence had
und sîn junchêrre Tristan.
and his young lord Tristan.

nu daz die vremeden koufman
when DEF-ART foreign merchants
[s Trading Ship, r 5]
ir market haeten ûz geleit,
their market had established,
vil schiere wart ze hove geseit,
quickly was at ZERO-ART court said
[idiomatic, also in English: *at court*]
waz dâ koufrâtes waere.
what there for sale was.
hier under kâmen maere
at the same time came ZERO-ART rumors
[s Parmenie, r 6]
Tristande z'unheile:
for Tristan ill luck:
dâ waeren valken veile
there were ZERO-ART falcons for sale
[s Market, r 6]
und ander schoene vederspil.
and other fine ZERO-ART birds of the chase.
[s Market, r 6]
und wart des maeres alsô vil,
and was of this rumor so much

biz zwei des marschalkes kint
that two of DEF-ART marshal sons
[s Parmenie, r 1]

(wan kint der dinge vlîzec sint)
(for ZERO-ART boys to such things are much given)
[s World, r 4]
under in zwein wurden in ein,
both two of them agreed
daz sî Tristanden zuo z'in zwein,
that they Tristan to them two,
ir wânbruoder, nâmen
their supposed brother, should take
und an ir vater kâmen
and to their father go

und bâten den bihanden,
and ask him at once
daz er in durch Tristanden
that he for them for Tristan's sake
der valken koufen hieze.
DEF-ART falcons to buy ordered.
[s Market, r 5]
der edele Rûal lieze
DEF-ART noble Rual would order [it]
[s Parmenie, r 1]
und haete ez nôte verlân,
and would it not leave undone,

ez enmüese allez vür sich gân,
it had all to happen,
des sîn vriunt Tristan baete,
what his friend Tristan asked for,
wan er in werder haete
for he him liked more
und bôt ez baz im einem
and treated better him alone

dan aller der dekeinem
than any other person

von lande oder von gesinde.
from ZERO-ART country or from servants.
[idiomatic; similar expressions:
8592 von lande und von gesten (Bechstein 1873:286),
8811 von lande zu lande (Bechstein 1873:293)]
sîner eigenen kinde
to his own sons
was er sô vlîzec niht sô sîn.
was he so not devoted.
dar an tete er der werlde schîn,
in this he to DEF-ART world showed,
[s World, r 1]
wie vollekomener triuwe er pflac,
what ZERO-ART perfect loyalty he had,
[s Marshal, r 6]

waz tugende und êren an im lac.
what ZERO-ART virtue and honor he possessed.
[s Marshal, r 6]
Er stuont ûf unde nam zehant
He rose and took at once
sînen sun Tristanden an die hant
his son Tristan by DEF-ART hand
[s Human, r 1]
nâch vil vaterlîchem site.
as it is for a father customary.
sîn ander süne giengen mite
his other sons went with them

und dar zuo hovegesindes vil,
and also of ZERO-ART retainers many,
[s Parmenie, r 4]
die sô durch ernest sô durch spil
who either seriously or for amusement

in volgeten unz an den kiel.
them followed down to DEF-ART keel,
[s Trading Ship, r 1]
und swaz ieman dâ geviel,
and whatever one there liked,
dâ in sîn wille zuo getruoc,
whatever one's fancy took,

des vant er umbe kouf genuoc.
of that found he for sale enough.
kleinoede, sîden, edele wât:
ZERO-ART jewels, silk, rich clothes,
[s Market, r 6]
des was dâ rât über rât.
of it was there a plentiful store.
ouch was dâ schoene vederspil,
also were there ZERO-ART fine hunting birds
[s Market, r 6]
valken pilgerîne vil,
falcons peregrines many,

smirlîne und sperwaere,
merlins and sparrowhawks
habeche mûzaere
hawks that had mewed
und ouch in rôten vederen:
and also with ZERO-ART red feathers:
[s Market, r 6]
von disen ietwederen
of all these
vant man vollen market dâ.
found one ample market there.

Tristande hiez man koufen sâ
For Tristan was ordered to buy at once
valken unde smirlîn.
ZERO-ART falcons and merlins.
[s Market, r 4]

die sîne bruoder solten sîn,
those who his brothers were thought to be,
den wart ouch dâ gekouft durch in.
for them also there were bought [birds] for his sake.
man gewan in allen drin,
was obtained for all three,

Swes iegelîcher gerte.
whatever each wished for
Nu man sî dô gewerte
Now that they were given
alles, des sî wolten,
all that they wanted
und dannen kêren solten,
and from there were about to turn back
von âventiure ez dô geschach,
accidentally it there happened

daz Tristan in dem schiffe ersach
that Tristan in DEF-ART ship noticed
[s Trading Ship, r 1]
ein schâchzabel hangen,
INDEF-ART chessboard hanging
[s Trading Ship, r 2]
an brete und an den spangen
with ZERO-ART wood and with DEF-ART clasps
[s Chessboard, r 6] [s Chessboard, r 5]
vil schône und wol gezieret,
very beautiful and well decorated
ze wunsche gefeitieret.
perfectly embellished.

The main mental spaces in the fragment are Parmenie, Trading Ship, and Market. The first two are introduced at the beginning of the text:

(2150 r) …*ein koufschif unde dekeinez mê*
one trading ship, and no more

in daz lant ze Parmenîe kam
to DEF-ART country of Parmenie came
[s World, r 1]

The following part contains alternating references to both mental spaces:

(2155 r) daz selbe castêl,
that same castle,
dâ der marschalc ze staete
where DEF-ART marshal always
[s Parmenie, r 1]
sîn wesen ûfe haete
his residence had

Der marschalc 'DEF-ART marshal' is referred to several times, always with a definite NP:

(2165 r) und wart des maeres alsô vil,
and was of this rumor so much
biz zwei des marschalkes kint...
that two of DEF-ART marshal sons
[s Parmenie, r 1]

(2175 r) der edele Rûal lieze
DEF-ART noble Rual would order [it]
[s Parmenie, r 1]
und haete ez nôte verlân,
and would it not leave undone,

The merchants who arrived on the trading ship are part of the instantiated frame: the first reference to them occurs with a definite article. The same sentence introduces the third major mental space of the fragment—Market:

(2160 r) nu daz die vremeden koufman
when DEF-ART foreign merchants
[s Trading Ship, r 5]
ir market haeten ûz geleit...
their market had established...

New elements are added to the MS Market using nouns with zero article, as formulated in Rule 6:

(2165 r) dâ waeren valken veile
there were ZERO-ART falcons for sale
[s Market, r 6]
und ander schoene vederspil.
and other fine ZERO-ART birds of the chase.
[s Market, r 6]

(2195–2200 r) *dâ in sîn wille zuo getruoc,*
whatever one's fancy took,
des vant er umbe kouf genuoc.
of that found he for sale enough.
kleinoede, sîden, edele wât:
ZERO-ART jewels, silk, rich clothes,
[s Market, r 6]

The space Trading Ship includes a default element of the frame Ship *den kiel* 'DEF-ART keel'. The reference to it can also be viewed as an instance of metonymy:

(2195 r) ...die sô durch ernest sô durch spil
who either seriously or for amusement
in volgeten unz an den kiel...
them followed down to DEF-ART keel
[s Trading Ship, r 1]

Much later in the fragment the ship is mentioned again. The definite article confirms that the referent of the noun is the same object as the one introduced previously:

(2215–2220 r) ...von âventiure ez dô geschach,
accidentally it there happened
daz Tristan in dem schiffe ersach
that Tristan in DEF-ART ship noticed
[s Trading Ship, r 1]
ein schâchzabel hangen,
INDEF-ART chessboard hanging
[s Trading Ship, r 2]

5.3 Early New High German

We shall examine the use of articles in excerpts from two texts representing the Early New High German period: *The Memoirs of Helene Kottanner*, composed in 1439–1440, and *Mentelin's Bible*, published in 1466.

Die Denkwürdigkeiten der Helene Kottannerin (Mollay 1971:11–13)
The Memoirs of Helene Kottanner

1. Do nu das geschehen was,
When now that happened,
da sandt meiner fraun gnad zu graf Jorgen von Posing
then sent my gracios lady to count Jorgen of Posing
vnd vordert die Slussel
and demanded DEF-ART keys
[s Plintenburg Castle, r 5]
zu der Plintenpurg , das wolten
to DEF-ART Plintenburg, because wanted
[s Plintenburg Castle, r 1]
die Vngrischen herren also haben,
DEF-ART Hungarian lords also
[s Hungary, r 5]
daz si das Gslos solt Ingeben irem Vettern,
that she DEF-ART castle should entrust to her cousin,
[s Plintenburg Castle, r 1]
herrn Laslawan von Gara .
lord Ladislaus of Gara.
2. Das geschach also.
This happened also.
3. Her Laslawan von Gara
Lord Ladislaus of Gara
nam das Gslos in vnd
took DEF-ART castle and
[s Plintenburg Castle, r 1]
besaczt das mit ainem purggrafen.
appointed there INDEF-ART castellan.
[s Plintenburg Castle, r 2]
4. Do nu die edel Kuniginn wolt
Then as DEF-ART noble queen wanted
[s Hungary, r 1]

wider gen Ofen ziehen mit
again to Ofen go with
irm vetter Lasslawan vnd mit den andern Vngrischen herren,
her cousin Ladislaus and with DEF-ART other Hungarian lords,
[s Hungary, r 5]
do nam mich ir gnad in ir gehaim vnd sprach:
then confided to me her grace her secret and said:
5. *"liebe vnd getrewe Quottannerin,*
"dear and faithful Kottanner,
lasst euch mein tochter enpholhen sein,
watch over my daughter,
vnd auch die kamer, da laszt nyemt ingen
and also DEF-ART room, there allow nobody to enter
[s Plintenburg Castle, r 1]
Dann mein tochter vnd ir."
Except my daughter and you."
6. *Vnd enphalch mir auch ir kran*
And entrusted to me also her crown
vnd ir halspant vnd ander ir klainat,
and her necklace and other her jewels,
das het ich alles in derselben kamer,
that had I all in the same room,
da durch man Ingieng
through which one passed [to get]
zu der Heiligen kron.
to DEF-ART Holy Crown.
[s Hungary, r 1]
7. *Vnd do wir also mit einander redten,*
And as we now with each other spoke,
do kam her Laslawan vnd auch sein purggraue, vnd sprach:
then came lord Ladislaus and also his castellan, and said:
8. *"gnedige fraw, ir solt mit der fraun schaffen,*
"gracious lady, you should with DEF-ART lady arrange,
[s Room, r 1]
daz si nympt in dew Kamer lasz, vnd auch meinen
that she nobody in DEF-ART room allows, and also not my
[s Plintenburg Castle, r 1]
purkgrafen".
castellan".

9. Do ward ir gnad guetlich antburtten vnd sprach zu mir:
Then her grace wisely responded and spoke to me:
10. "liebe Helena Quottannerin, wann mein veter,
"dear Helene Kottanner, when my cousin,
her Laslawan vnd sein purkgraf
her Ladislaus, and his castellan
herinwellen, so laszt sie herin."
want to go inside, let them in."
11. Do gie der purggraf
Then went DEF-ART castellan
[s Plintenburg Castle, r 1]
zu der tur, do die sigel an waren,
to DEF-ART door, on which DEF-ART seals were,
[s Room, r 1] [s Door, r 5]
vnd nam ain tüehel vnd legt es vber
and took INDEF-ART piece of cloth and put it over
[s Room, r 2]
dy sigel vnd pant das tuehel zu
DEF-ART seals and tied DEF-ART piece of cloth [into a knot]
[s Door, r 5] [s Door, r 1]
vnd legat sein sigel darauf.
and pressed his seal on it.
12. Da das alles geschach,
When this all happened,
da schied die edel witib vnd mein gnedige fraw
then rode off DEF-ART noble widow and my gracious lady
[s Hungary, r1]
mit ierm Vettern, her laslawan,
with her cousin, lord Ladislaus,
vnd mit den andern vngrischen herren da hin gen Ofen ,
and with DEF-ART other Hungarian lords to Ofen,
[s Hungary, r 5]
vberladen mit ainer sweren purd, vnd vmbgeben
troubled by INDEF-ART heavy burden, and beset
[s Queen, r 2]
mit vil sorgen, Wann die vngrischen herren
by many worries, bcause DEF-ART Hungarian lords
[s Hungary, r 5]

die wolten nur, Si solt ainen man nemen,
they wanted only, she should INDEF-ART husband take,
[s Marriage, r 2]
vnd hielten iren gnaden ettleich fur, vnd was
and proposed to her grace several [candidates], and was
ainer der Kung von Polan , genant her
one DEF-ART King of Poland, named lord
[s Poland, r 1]
Bladislaus , der ander
Wladislaus, the other
des Dispoten sun aus der Sirfey.
of DEF-ART despot son from DEF-ART Serbia.
[s Serbia, r 1] [s World, r 1]
13. Darumb was die edel KungInn vast betruebt
Because of that was DEF-ART noble Queen very troubled
[s Hungary, r 1]
vnd vnder ander Hofleicher antburt sprach Si also:
and among other courteous answers said she also:
14. "Lieben herren, gebt mir nicht ainen Haiden,
"Dear lords, give me not INDEF-ART pagan,
[s Marriage, r 2]
gebt mier lieber ainen kristenpauren.
give me instead INDEF-ART Christian peasant.
[s Marriage, r 2]
15. "Vnd da wolt herr Laslawan, ir veter,
"And then wanted lord Ladislaus, her cousin,
Si solt den von Polan nemmen.
she should the one from Poland take.
16. Do stuenden die Vngrischen herren all auf,
Then insisted DEF-ART Hungarian lords all,
[s Hungary, r 5]
daz Si das tuen solt,
that she that do should,
17. Aber Si wolt nicht vnd gab zu antburtt, Si wolt
but she wanted not and answered, she wanted
wartten, was ir got geb, dar nach wolt
to wait, what her God would give, accordingly wanted
Si sich richten.
she to decide.

18. Wann ir heten all ir Arczt gesagt,
For her had all her doctors told,
Si trueg ainen Sun, vnd des hiet Si hofnung,
she was carrying INDEF-ART son, and that gave her hope,
[s Pregnancy, r 2]
19. Aber Si mocht der warhait nicht wissen vnd
but she could DEF-ART truth not know and
[s Pregnancy, r 5]
mocht sich darnach nicht richten, vnd da hueb
could accordingly not decide, and then left
sich ir gnad ubring auf von Ofen Vnd fur wider
her grace again Ofen and moved back
zu der Plintenpurg vnden in den Hof.
to DEF-ART Plintenburg and to DEF-ART court.
[s Plintenburg Castle, r 1] [s Plintenburg Castle, r 1]
20. Da kam graf Vlrich von Zily zu ir,
Then came count Ulrich of Zily to her,
des wuerden die Vngrischen herren Inne,
this DEF-ART Hungarian lords learned,
[s Hungary, r 5]
vnd komen pald her nach zu iern gnaden,
and came soon after to her grace,
vnd drungen Si aber an von des von Polan wegen.
and bothered her again because of [the King of] Poland.
21. Do ward ir geraten, Si solt sich willigen den von
Then she was advised, she should agree the one from
Polan zenemen, vnd solt die weil trachten,
Poland to take, and should in the meantime pursue,
was ir das peste were, man wurd
what for her the best was, one would
dannoch wol ainen sin vinden,
later easily INDEF-ART reason find,
[s Marriage, r 2]
daz Si davon kem
to get out of her promise
22. vnd tet ir gnad vnd willigat sich,
and did [this] her grace and agree,
den von Polan zenemen.
the one from Poland to marry.

23. Aber doch hielt Si in drey sach fur,
However stated she ZERO-ART three things,
[s Marriage, r 6]
die man
which [every]one
wol wais, ob sie das halten wolten, so wolt Si
well knows, if they them to fulfill agreed, then would she
den von Polan nemen.
the one from Poland marry.
24. Aber Si wessat wol, daz sy
But she knew well, that they
der dreirr artikel kainen hielten,
of DEF-ART three conditions none could satisfy,
[s Marriage, r 5]
vnd wolt damit ausgen aus der willigung,
and wanted in this manner to get out of DEF-ART promise,
[s Marriage, r 1]
die Sie getan het, den von Polan zunemen.
which she had made, the one from Poland to marry.
25. Das verstuenden die herren nicht vnd
That understood DEF-ART lords not and
[s Hungary, r 5]
waren fro, daz sich ir gnad gewilligt het,
were glad, that her grace agreed,
den von Polan zenemen.
the one from Poland to marry.
26. Da das dy weis vnd die edel KungInn verstund,
Since this DEF-ART wise and noble queen understood,
[s Hungary, r 1]
do ward Si gedenkchen vnd trachten
she thought and strived
nach der Heiligen kron, wie Si die in ir gewalt
for DEF-ART Holy Crown, how she it in her possession
[s Hungary, r 1]
mocht bringen von den vngrischen herren.
could bring from DEF-ART Hungarian lords.
[s Hungary, r 5]
27. Das tet Si auf die maynung,
That did she because of DEF-ART consideration,
[s Pregnancy, r 1]

ob das wer, daz Si
that if it happened, that she
ainen Sun geperet, daz der
to INDEF-ART son gave birth, that he
[s Pregnancy, r 2]
von dem Reich nicht wurd verdrungen,
from DEF-ART kingdom would not be ousted,
[s Hungary, r 1]
trueg Si aber ain tochter, so mocht Si dennoch
if she gave birth to INDEF-ART daughter, then could she still
[s Pregnancy, r 2]
dester pas ainer taiding bekomen
because of that better INDEF-ART judgment receive
[s Hungary, r 2]
von den vngrischen herren Vnd pat mich vast, ob ich
from DEF-ART Hungarian lords and asked me firmly, whether I
[s Hungary, r 5]
die Heiligen Kron heraws mocht bringen...
DEF-ART Holy Crown could bring
[s Hungary, r 1]
28. Da hieten die Vngrischen herren gern gesehen,
Then DEF-ART Hungarian lords would prefer,
[s Hungary, r 5]
daz die edel kunginn
that DEF-ART noble queen
[s Hungary, r 1]
auf der Plintenpurig
in DEF-ART Plintenburg
[s Plintenburg Castle, r 1]
in der kindelpett wer gelegen.
in DEF-ART childbirth bed would lie.
[s Pregnancy, r 1]

The first mental space in the fragment is the Plintenburg Castle. One of the default elements of the corresponding frame—*die Slussel* 'DEF-ART keys' is introduced with the definite article:

(1 r) da sandt meiner fraun gnad zu graf Jorgen von Posing
then sent my gracios lady to count Jorgen of Posing

vnd vordert die Slussel
and demanded DEF-ART keys
[s Plintenburg Castle, r 5]
zu der Plintenpurg , das wolten
to DEF-ART Plintenburg
[s Plintenburg Castle, r 1]

In the following sentences the word *Gslos* 'castle' is used. The definite article confirms that the noun refers to the same entity:

(1 r) ...wolten die Vngrischen herren also haben,
...wanted DEF-ART Hungarian lords also
daz si das Gslos solt Ingeben irem Vettern
that she DEF-ART castle should entrust to her cousin
[s Plintenburg Castle, r 1]

A new entity *ainem purggrafen* 'INDEF-ART castellan' is added to the mental space with an indefinite article. A reference with a definite article follows:

(3 r) Her Laslawan von Gara
Lord Ladislaus of Gara
nam das Gslos in vnd
took DEF-ART castle and
[s Plintenburg Castle, r 1]
besaczt das mit ainem purggrafen.
appointed there INDEF-ART castellan.
[s Plintenburg Castle, r 2]

(11 r) Do gie der purggraf
Then went DEF-ART castellan
[s Plintenburg Castle, r 1]
zu der tur...
to DEF-ART door

At the time of the narrative, the Holy Crown of Hungary was stored in one of the rooms in the Plintenburg Castle:

(6 r) ...das het ich alles in derselben kamer,
that had I all in the same room,

da durch man Ingieng
hrough which one passed [to get]
zu der Heiligen kron.
to DEF-ART Holy Crown.
[s Hungary, r 1]

(8 r) "gnedige fraw, ir solt mit der fraun schaffen,
"gracious lady, you should with DEF-ART lady arrange,
daz si nympt in dew Kamer lasz...
that she nobody into DEF-ART room allows
[s Plintenburg Castle, r 1]

A default element of the frame Room—*tur* 'door'—is referred to using a definite NP:

(11 r) Do gie der purggraf
Then went DEF-ART castellan
zu der tur
to DEF-ART door
[s Room, r 1]

All entities in the mental space Hungary are default elements of the frame Country and therefore all references to them are definite NPs: *die edel Kuniginn* 'DEF-ART noble queen', *der Heiligen kron* 'DEF-ART Holy Crown', *die edel witib* 'DEF-ART noble widow' (referring to the queen), *dem Reich* 'DEF-ART kingdom'. Below are the corresponding fragments:

(4 r) Do nu die edel Kuniginn wolt
Then as DEF-ART noble queen wanted
[s Hungary, r 1]
wider gen Ofen ziehen
again to Ofen to go

(6 r) das het ich alles in derselben kamer,
that had I all in the same room,
da durch man Ingieng
through which one passed [to get]
zu der Heiligen kron.
to DEF-ART Holy Crown.
[s Hungary, r 1]

(12 r) da schied die edel witib vnd mein gnedige fraw
then rode off DEF-ART noble widow and my gracious lady
[s Hungary, r1]
da hin gen Ofen
to Ofen

(26 r) Da das dy weis vnd die edel KungInn verstund,
Since this DEF-ART wise and noble queen understood,
[s Hungary, r 1]
do ward Si gedenkchen vnd trachten
she thought and strived
nach der Heiligen kron...
for DEF-ART Holy Crown
[s Hungary, r 1]

(27 r) ob das wer,
that if it happened,
daz Si ainen Sun geperet, daz der
that she to INDEF-ART son gave birth, that he
von dem Reich nicht wurd verdrungen
from DEF-ART kingdom would not be ousted
[s Hungary, r 1]

The frame Pregnancy is represented by *ainen Sun* 'INDEF-ART son', *ain tochter* 'INDEF-ART daughter', *der kindelpett* 'DEF-ART childbirth bed'. *Der kindelpett* refers to a default element of the frame and therefore has a definite article:

(27 r) ob das wer,
that if it happened,
daz Si ainen Sun geperet, daz der
that she to INDEF-ART son gave birth, that he
[s Pregnancy, r 2]
von dem Reich nicht wurd verdrungen,
from DEF-ART kingdom would not be ousted,
trueg Si aber ain tochter...
if she gave birth to INDEF-ART daughter
[s Pregnancy, r 2]

(28 r) Da hieten die Vngrischen herren gern gesehen,
Then DEF-ART Hungarian lords would prefer,

daz die edel kunginn
that DEF-ART noble queen
auf der Plintenpurig
in DEF-ART Plintenburg
in der kindelpett wer gelegen.
in DEF-ART childbirth bed would lie.
[s Pregnancy, r 1]

Die erste deutsche Bibel (Kurrelmeyer 1904:381–385)
The first German Bible

Iohannes 11
John 11

1. *Wann ein ſiecher lazarus was von bethania:*
Now INDEF-ART ailing [man] Lazarus was from Bethany:
[s Bethany, r 2]
von dem caſtelle marine vnd marthen ir ſchweſter.
from DEF-ART village of Mary and Martha her sister
[s Judea, r 1]

2. *Wann maria waz die do ſielb den herren*
and Mary was the one who anointed DEF-ART lord
[s World, r 1]
mit der ſalben vnd trucket ſein fúß mit iren haren:
with DEF-ART fragrant oil and wiped His feet with her hair
[s The House of the Pharisee, r 5]
der bruder lazarus ſiecht.
her brother Lazarus was sick.

3. *Dorumb ſein ſchweſtern ſantten*
So his sisters sent
zu im ſagent. O herre: ſich den du liebhaſt der ſiecht.
to Him saying Lord look the one You love he is sick.

4. *Wann do es iheſus gehort: er ſprach zu in.*
When it Jesus heard he spoke to them
Dirr ſiechtumb iſt nit zu dem tod
This sickness is not to [end in] DEF-ART death
[s Life, r 1]

wann vmb die wunniglich gotz:
but for DEF-ART glory of God
[s God, r 1]
das der ſun gotz werd gewunniglicht durch in.
so that DEF-ART Son of God will be glorified through it.
[s World, r 1]

5. *Wann iheſus het lieb marthen vnd marien*
And Jesus loved Martha and Mary
ir ſchweſter vnd lazarum.
her sister and Lazarus.

6. *Dorumb do er het gehort das er ſiecht:*
So when He heard that he is sick
ernſtlich do beleyb er an der ſelben ſtat zwen tage.
indeed then remained he in the same place ZERO-ART two days.
[s Stay at the Jordan, r 6]

7. *Dornach nach diſen dingen ſprach er*
Then after these things spoke he
zu ſeinen iungern. Wir gen aber in iude
to his disciples. We go again to Judea

8. *Die iungern ſprachen zu im. Meyſter nu ſuchten dich*
DEF-ART disciples spoke to him master now were seeking you
[s Stay at the Jordan, r 5]
die iuden zeſteinen: vnd aber geſtu dar?
DEF-ART Jews to stone and again you go there?
[s Judea, r 5]

9. *Iheſus antwurt. Seint nit xij stunde des tags?*
Jesus answered Are not twelve hours of DEF-ART day?
[s Day, r 1]
Der do get am tag der ſchat nit:
The one who walks in DEF-ART day he stumbles not
[s Day, r 1]
wann er ſicht das liecht dirr werlt.
because he sees DEF-ART light of this world
[s Day, r 1]

10. Wann ob er geet in der nacht er ſchat:
Now if he goes in DEF-ART night he stumbles:
[s Day, r 1]
wann das liech iſt nit in im.
because DEF-ART light is not in him.
[s Day, r 1]

11. Wann ditz ſagt er:
Now this said he
vnd dornach ſprach er zu in. Lazarus vnſer freunt der
and then spoke he to them Lazarus our friend he
ſchleft wann ich gee daz ich in derſte
is asleep and I go so that I him awake
von dem ſchlaff.
from DEF-ART sleep.
[s Life, r 5]

12. Dorumb ſein iungern die ſprachen.
Therefore his disciples they spoke
O herr: ob er ſleft er wirt behalten.
Lord, if he is asleep he will be saved

13. Wann iheſus hett geſait von ſeim tode:
But Jesus had spoken about his death
wann ſy wonten das er hett geſait von
but they thought that he had spoken of
dem ſchlaff des ſlaffes
DEF-ART sleep of DEF-ART sleep.
[s Life, r 5] [s Life, r 5]

14. Do ſprach iheſus zu in
Then spoke Jesus to them
offenlich Lazarus der iſt dott:
freely Lazarus he is dead

15. wann ich frewe mich vmb euch das ir glaubt:
but I rejoice for your sake that you may believe
das ich do nichten was. Wann wir geen zu im.
that I was not there but we go to him.

16. Dorumb thomas der ift gefait
Therefore Thomas who is called
ein zweifeler der fprach
INDEF-ART twin he spoke
[s Stay at the Jordan, r 2; cf. discussion of the construct *DEF-ART N1 is INDEF-ART N2* in Section 3.2]
zu den entzampt iungern. Geen auch wir:
to DEF-ART other disciples. Let us go also
[s Stay at the Jordan, r 5]
vnd fterben mit im.
and die with him.

17. Dorumb ihefus kam in bethania:
Then Jesus came to Bethany
vnd vand in ietzunt iiij tag habent im grabe.
and found him already ZERO-ART four days in DEF-ART tomb.
[s Death, r 6] [s Death, r 1]

18. Wann bethania was von iherufalem als
Now Bethany was from Jerusalem
xv leuff
ZERO-ART fifteen stadia away
[s Bethany, r 6]

19. Wann manig von den iuden die kamen zu
And many of DEF-ART Jews they came to
[s Judea, r 5]
mariam vnd zu marthen: das fy fy troften
Mary and to Martha so that they them comfort
von irem bruder
because of their brother.

20. Dorumb do martha gehort
Now when Martha heard
daz ihefus kam fy lieff im entgegen:
that Jesus came she ran to meet him
wann maria faß do heim.
but Mary was sitting at home.

21. Dorumb martha fprach zu ihefus.
Now Martha spoke to Jesus

O herr ob du werſt hie geweſt mein bruder
Lord if you were here my brother
der wer nit dott.
he would not be dead.

22. Wann ioch nu weyß ich das:
But even now know I that
was dings du eiſcht von gott gibt dir gott.
what you ask of God will give you God

23. Iheſus ſprach zu ir. Dein bruder der derſtet.
Jesus spoke to her your brother will rise again.

24. Martha ſprach zu im. Ich waiß das er derſtet
Martha spoke to him. I know that he will rise again
in der aufferſtendung an dem iungſten tag.
in DEF-ART resurrection at DEF-ART last day.
[s Life, r 1] [s World, r 1]

25. Iheſus ſprach zu ir. Ich bin die aufferſtendung
Jesus spoke to her. I am DEF-ART resurrection
[s Life, r 1]
vnd das leben. Der an mich gelaubet ioch
and DEF-ART life. He who believes in me even
[s Life, r 1]
ob er wer dott er lebt:
if he were dead he shall live

26. vnd ein ieglicher der do lebt vnd an mich gelaubt:
and everyone who lives and in me believes
der ſtirbt nit ewiglich Gelaubſtu das.
he shall not die ever Do you believe this

27. Sy ſprach zu im O herr ia. Ich glaub daz du biſt
She spoke to him Lord yes I believe that you are
criſtus der ſun gotz des lebentigen:
Christ DEF-ART son of God the living:
[s World, r 1]
du do biſt kumen in diſe werlt.
you who has come in this world.

28. Vnd do ſy ditz hett geſait: ſy gieng hin
And when she this had said she went away
vnd rieff marine ir ſchweſter tugetlich ſagent.
and called Mary her sister secretly saying
Der maiſter iſt en gegenwurtig: vnd ruft dir.
DEF-ART teacher has come and is calling for you
[s Bethany, r 1]

29. Wann do ſis gehort ſy stund auf ſchier: vnd kam zu im
When she that heard she got up quickly and came to him.

30. Wann iheſus was dennoch nit kumen in das caſtel:
Now Jesus had not yet come into DEF-ART village
[s Bethany, r 1]
wann er was noch an der ſtat do im martha begegnet.
but he was still at DEF-ART place where him Martha had met
[s Bethany, r 1]

31. Dorumb die iuden die mit ir warn im haus
When DEF-ART Jews who with her were in DEF-ART house
[s House, r 5] [s House, r 1]
vnd ſy troſten do ſy geſachen das maria
and her comforted when they saw that Mary
ſchier aufſtund vnd gieng auß: ſy nachuolgten ir ſagent.
quickly got up and went out they followed her saying
Wann ſy geet zu dem grab daz ſy do waint
that she went to DEF-ART tomb so that she there weeps
[s Tomb, r 1]

32. Wann do maria was kumen do iheſus waz:
When then Mary came where Jesus was
Do ſy in geſach ſy viel zu ſeinen füſſen vnd ſprach zu im.
when she him saw she fell down at his feet and spoke to him
O herr ob du werſt hie geweſt mein bruder wer nit dott.
Lord if you were here my brother would not be dead

33. Wann iheſus ſach ſy wainen vnd die iuden
When Jesus saw her weeping and DEF-ART Jews
[s House, r 5]
die do warn kumen mit ir die wainten er griſgrampt
who there were came with her they were weeping he groaned

im geiſt: vnd betreubt ſich ſelber vnd ſprach
in DEF-ART spirit and troubled himself and spoke
[s Human, r 1]

34. Wo habt ir in gelegt? Sy ſprachen zu im.
Where have you laid him? They spoke to him
O herr kum vnd ſieh.
Lord come and see.

35. Vnd iheſus waint.
And Jesus wept.

36. Dorumb die iuden ſprachen. Secht wie lieb er in hat.
Therefore DEF-ART Jews spoke look how loved he him.
[s House, r 5]

37. Wann etlich von in die ſprachen. Der do aufdet
And certain of them they spoke The one who opened
die augen des blinden geborn: mocht er nit gethun
DEF-ART eyes of DEF-ART blind born could he not make
[s Human, r 5] [s Jerusalem, r 1]
das dirr nicht wer geſtorben?
that this [man] not would have died?

38. Dorumb iheſus griſgrampt anderwaid in im ſelber
Therefore Jesus groaned again in himself
er kam zu dem grabe.
he came to DEF-ART tomb
[s Tomb, r 1]
Wann es was ein grub
and it was INDEF-ART cave
[s Tomb, r 2]
vnd ein ſtaine
and INDEF-ART stone
[s Tomb, r 2]
was dorauuff gelegt.
was upon it placed.

39. Iheſus ſprach. Hebt ab den ſtain
Jesus spoke take away DEF-ART stone
[s Tomb, r 1]

Martha die ſchewſter des der do waz dot die ſprach
Martha DEF-ART sister of the one who there was dead she spoke
[s Tomb, r 1]
zu im o herr er ſmeckt ietzunt:
to him Lord there is a bad odor now
wann er iſt iiij tegig.
for he has been there four days.

40. Iheſus ſprach zu ir.
Jesus spoke to her
Sait ich dir denn nit: ob du gelaubſt du ſichſt
Said I to you not if you believe you shall see
die wuniglich gotz?
DEF-ART glory of God
[s God, r 1]

41. Dorumb ſy namen ab den ſtain.
So they took away DEF-ART stone
[s Tomb, r 1]
Iheſus hub auff die augen in den himel er ſprach.
Jesus lifted DEF-ART eyes to DEF-ART heaven he spoke
[s Human, r 5] [s World, r 1]
O vatter ich mache dir genad wann du derhorteſt mich.
Father I thank you because you heard me

42. Wann ich waiß das du mich zeallen zeyten
And I know that you me always
derhorst: wann vmb das volck daz alumb ſtet
will hear but because of DEF-ART multitude that is standing by
[s Tomb, r 5]
ich ſprach das ſy glauben das du mich ſanteſt.
I spoke so that they believe that you me sent.

43. Do er ditz hett geſait: er rieff
When he that had said he cried out
mit einer micheln ſtymme.
with INDEF-ART loud voice
[s Tomb, r 2]
Lazare kum herfúr.
Lazarus come forth

44. Vnd zehand fürgieng der der do was dott
And at once came forth he who there was dead

The news of Lazarus' death adds the frame Death to the set of mental spaces of the fragment. As an element of that frame, Lazarus' tomb is referred to with a definite NP at first mention:

(14 r) Do ſprach iheſus zu in
Then spoke Jesus to them
offenlich Lazarus der iſt dott:
freely Lazarus he is dead

(17 r) Dorumb iheſus kam in bethania:
Then Jesus came to Bethany
vnd vand in ietzunt
and found him already
iiij tag habent im grabe.
ZERO-ART four days in DEF-ART tomb.
[s Death, r 6] [s Death, r 1]

The events in the final part of the fragment occur at Lazarus' tomb:

(38 r) Dorumb iheſus griſgrampt anderwaid in im ſelber
Therefore Jesus groaned again in himself
er kam zu dem grabe.
he came to DEF-ART tomb
[s Tomb, r 1]

A new object—*ſtain* 'stone'— is added using an indefinite NP. Two definite references follow:

(38 r) Wann es was ein grub
and it was INDEF-ART cave
vnd ein ſtaine
and INDEF-ART stone
[s Tomb, r 2]
was dorauuff gelegt.
was upon it placed.

(39 r) Ihefus fprach. Hebt ab den ftain
Jesus spoke take away DEF-ART stone
[s Tomb, r 1]

(41 r) Dorumb fy namen ab den ftain.
So they took away DEF-ART stone
[s Tomb, r 1]

Default elements of the frame Day mentioned in the fragment include *des tags* 'DEF-ART day', *das liecht* 'DEF-ART light', *der nacht* 'DEF-ART night':

(9 r) Ihefus antwurt. Seint nit xij stunde des tags?
Jesus answered Are not twelve hours of DEF-ART day?
[s Day, r 1]
Der do get am tag der fchat nit:
The one who walks in DEF-ART day he stumbles not
[s Day, r 1]
wann er ficht das liecht dirr werlt.
because he sees DEF-ART light of this world
[s Day, r 1]

(10 r) Wann ob er geet in der nacht er fchat:
Now if he goes in DEF-ART night he stumbles:
[s Day, r 1]
wann das liech ift nit in im.
because DEF-ART light is not in him.
[s Day, r 1]

A number of nouns with a definite article correspond to default elements of the frame Human Life, e.g. *dem tod* 'DEF-ART death', *die aufferftendung* 'DEF-ART resurrection', *das leben* 'DEF-ART life':

(4 r) Dirr fiechtumb ift nit zu dem tod
This sickness is not to [end in] DEF-ART death
[s Life, r 1]

(25 r) Ihefus fprach zu ir. Ich bin die aufferftendung
Jesus spoke to her. I am DEF-ART resurrection
[s Life, r 1]

vnd *das leben.*
and DEF-ART life.
[s Life, r 1]

Default elements of the frame Human are also referred to using definite NPs, e.g. *im geiſt* 'in DEF-ART spirit', *die augen* 'DEF-ART eyes'

(33 r) Wann iheſus ſach ſy wainen...
When Jesus saw her weeping ...
er griſgrampt *im geiſt*
he groaned in DEF-ART spirit
[s Human, r 1]

(37 r) Wann etlich von in *die ſprachen.* *Der* *do aufdet*
And certain of them they spoke The one who opened
die augen *des blinden geborn*
DEF-ART eyes of DEF-ART blind born
[s Human, r 5]

(41 r) Iheſus hub auff *die augen in* *den himel*
Jesus lifted DEF-ART eyes to DEF-ART heaven
[s Human, r 5]

5.4 Evaluation of Results

In the analyzed OHG text fragments four general cases can be clearly identified:

1. Zero article before nouns that would have a definite article in Modern German. Such uses are due to the fact that development of the definite article was still in progress in OHG. One of the main characteristics of this development was expansion to include new classes of nouns—from concrete to abstract (Hodler 1954:9).
2. The definite article is used with nouns referring to objects that are unique in the world.
3. The definite article is used with nouns whose referents have the status ACTIVATED due to a previous explicit introduction. According to Gundel et al. (1993:275), in all such cases a demonstrative pronoun can be used instead, or the article can be interpreted as a

demonstrative pronoun, if the same form is used to represent both categories.

4. The definite article is used with nouns whose referents are UNIQUELY IDENTIFIABLE. This domain belongs to the articles alone. A definite article in this role cannot be substituted by or interpreted as a demonstrative pronoun.

Our analysis of the MHG and ENHG fragments has shown that, just as in Modern German, the choice of an article is determined by the composition of the mental space that contains the referent of the corresponding noun and by the type of the referent. Frames form the basis for most of the mental spaces analyzed. The definite article is common before nouns whose referent was introduced in a mental space only indirectly—via an instantiated frame.

References to different mental spaces in the analyzed fragments are often interleaved. The choice of articles in such cases remains consistent and is determined by what the hearer knew about the mental space last time when one of its elements was mentioned.

The choice between the indefinite and zero article before a sg. noun introducing a new entity in a mental space is determined by the type of the referent. Nouns with an indefinite article are also used to assign properties corresponding to a new concept to an object already present in a mental space, as described in Section 3.2.

The definite article is used not only with nouns referring to entities in frames which are abstractions of common surroundings of individuals, e.g. Castle, House, Room, but also with nouns corresponding to elements of knowledge structures consisting of concepts like Life, Death, Resurrection.

Our analysis has shown that the approach proposed in the present study can be successfully applied to explain uses of articles in texts from all major periods of the history of the German language. The concepts of a mental space, the type of a referent, and a frame appear to be central to a description of definiteness not only in Modern German, but in its historical variants as well.

• CHAPTER SIX •

Conclusion

Recent advances in theoretical knowledge and computational power have made Natural Language Processing and Information Retrieval one of the fastest developing branches of Information Technology and one of the main domains of the practical application of linguistic research. In keeping with these tendencies, the present study was an attempt to investigate a linguistic problem and to demonstrate how the obtained results can be used in an automated NLP system.

Using the concept of a mental space as an intermediate level between real situations and their representations in discourse, and an ontology which specifies types of referents relevant for the category of definiteness, we presented a set of eight uniform rules that describe the system of articles in English and German. The proposed rules formulate conditions determining the choice of the definite, indefinite and zero articles.

Our set of rules can be used to infer properties of mental spaces corresponding to a text based on the articles that occur in it. We have shown how analysis of determiners helps to recognize instances of coreference and to identify mental spaces that contain referents of nouns in sample sentences and in larger text fragments from English and German prose.

An article is most informative when a mental space contains default elements of one or several instantiated frames which results in the use of definite NPs without previous explicit introduction of their referents. In such cases a definite NP can confirm that a mental space is an instance of a frame which requires the presence of exactly one member of the category corresponding to the noun.

On the basis of the proposed approach to the analysis of determiners we developed an automated system for nominal reference resolution. The system consists of an implementation of an algorithm that uses the information expressed by the category of definiteness, a unification parser that recognizes both syntactic and semantic features of noun phrases, and a heuristic function for ordering representations of mental spaces. This system successfully distinguishes between instances of coreference and the introduction of new entities; it creates realistic and robust reference representations.

Finally, we applied the proposed approach to data from all historical variants of the German language. Occurrences of *dër (thër)* before nouns referring to elements of frames demonstrate that the simple demonstrative pronoun was used to express definiteness—and not anaphora or deixis alone—already in OHG. We have also shown that the presented set of rules can be successfully used to analyze MHG and ENHG texts.

Implementation of the Algorithm for Nominal Reference Resolution

Below are the data structures and major functions used in our implementation of the algorithm, in pseudocode:

data structures:

mental-space, represents MSs encountered in the text

fields:

name, the noun that caused creation of this *mental-space*
name-group, the *frame-add* list
id, an index in the *ment-spaces* vector
initial, noun-id of the *name*
elements, lists of *noun-ids* of elements of this *mental-space*

noun-id, contains indices that identify a noun in the text

fields:

sent-index, index of the sentence that contains this noun
in-sent-index, index of the noun in the sentence
noun-index, index of the noun in the *noun-ids-seen* vector

global variables:

ment-spaces, a vector of *mental-space* data structures
noun-ids-seen, a vector containing *noun-ids* of all nouns in a text
noun-parses-seen, , a vector containing LFs of all nouns in a text
feat-lst-buffer, a vector for storing LFs of nouns from the current sentence
no-new-space, a flag to signal whether a new *mental-space* should be created

Figure A.1: Data structures and global variables.

The top-level function REFERENCE-REPRESENTATION computes a parse of each sentence and calls PROCESS-FEAT-LST-BUFFER. When REFERENCE-REPRESENTATION finishes execution, the vector *ment-spaces* will contain representations of referents of all nouns in the text, organized in *mental-space* data structures.

```
function REFERENCE-REPRESENTATION(text)
    inputs: text, a list of sentences, each of which is a list of words
    for each sentence cur-sent in text do
        cur-parse ← PARSE-NOUNS(cur-sent)
        sent-index ← GET-SENT-IND()
        when not null cur-parse
            in-sent-index ← 0
            for each feat-lst in cur-parse do
                noun-index ← GET-NOUN-IND()
                SET-INDICES(noun-ids-seen[noun-index],
                            sent-index, in-sent-index, noun-index)
                add [feat-lst | noun-index] to the end of feat-lst-buffer
                noun-parses-seen[noun-index] ← feat-lst
                increment in-sent-index
            PROCESS-FEAT-LST-BUFFER()
        increment sent-index
```

Figure A.2: REFERENCE-REPRESENTATION.

PROCESS-FEAT-LST-BUFFER moves LFs marked as *possible-frame-ref* to the front, calls HANDLE-NOUN-FEAT-LST with each LF in the buffer and takes a majority vote once *mental-space*s have been chosen.

```
function PROCESS-FEAT-LST-BUFFER()
    ORDER- FEAT-LST-BUFFER()
    for each buf-entry in feat-lst-buffer do
        HANDLE-NOUN-FEAT-LST(FIRST(buf-entry),
                             noun-ids-seen[SECOND(buf-entry)])
    TAKE-MAJORITY-VOTE ()
    feat-lst-buffer ← []
```

Figure A.3: PROCESS-FEAT-LST-BUFFER.

HANDLE-NOUN-FEAT-LST and HANDLE-FRAME-REF-FEAT-LST are simple dispatchers:

```
function HANDLE-NOUN-FEAT-LST (feat-lst n-id)
    inputs: feat-lst, the current LF
            n-id, a noun-id structure representing the current noun
    if MEMBER("possible-frame-ref", feat-lst)
        HANDLE-FRAME-REF-FEAT-LST (feat-lst n-id)
    else HANDLE-REG-FEAT-LST (feat-lst n-id)

function HANDLE-FRAME-REF-FEAT-LST (feat-lst n-id)
    inputs: feat-lst, the current LF
            n-id, a noun-id structure representing the current noun
    when not HANDLE-KNOWN-FRAME-REF(feat-lst n-id)
        HANDLE-NEW-FRAME-REF (feat-lst n-id)
```

Figure A.4: HANDLE-NOUN-FEAT-LST and HANDLE-FRAME-REF-FEAT-LST.

HANDLE-KNOWN-FRAME-REF sets the global flag *no-new-space* to *false* and returns its value after a call to HANDLE-REG-FEAT-LST. The function ADD-KNOWN-DEF-ELT, that may be called by HANDLE-REG-FEAT-LST, can set the flag to *true* as it executes.

```
function HANDLE-KNOWN-FRAME-REF (feat-lst n-id)
    inputs: feat-lst, the current LF
            n-id, a noun-id structure representing the current noun
    no-new-space ← false
    HANDLE-REG-FEAT-LST (feat-lst n-id)
    return no-new-space
```

Figure A.5: HANDLE-KNOWN-FRAME-REF.

HANDLE-NEW-FRAME-REF creates a new *mental-space* and adds it to *ment-spaces*

function HANDLE-NEW-FRAME-REF (*feat-lst n-id*)
inputs: *feat-lst,* the current LF
n-id, a *noun-id* structure representing the current noun
local variables: *new-space*, a *mental-space* data structure
new-space ← MAKE-MENT-SPACE()
new-space.name ← GET-NAME(*feat-lst*)
new-space.name-group ← GET-FRAME-ADD(*feat-lst*)
new-space.id ← GET-SPACE-ID()
new-space.initial ← *n-id*
new-space.elements ← [*n-id*]
ment-spaces[*id*] ← *new-space*

Figure A.6: HANDLE-NEW-FRAME-REF.

If an LF is not marked as *possible-frame-ref* it is processed by HANDLE-REG-FEAT-LST. This function uses our heuristic to order a fixed number of most recent *mental-spaces* by likelihood of their association with the current LF, and then calls ADD-USING-DETERMINERS to choose among them.

function HANDLE-REG-FEAT-LST (*feat-lst n-id*)
inputs: *feat-lst,* the current LF
n-id, a *noun-id* structure representing the current noun
local variables: *space-ids,* a list of ids of known MSs
space-ids ← GET-SPACE-IDS(*ment-spaces*)
ORDER-USING-FIND-CLOSEST (*space-ids feat-lst n-id*)
ADD-USING-DETERMINERS (*space-ids feat-lst n-id*)

Figure A.7: HANDLE-REG-FEAT-LST.

If the current LF is marked as definite, ADD-USING-DETERMINERS calls ADD-KNOWN-DEF-ELT with several *mental-spaces* (ordered in the previous step). Otherwise only the first *mental-space* is considered.

```
function ADD-USING-DETERMINERS (feat-lst space-ids n-id)
    inputs: feat-lst, the current LF
            space-ids, an ordered list of indices in ment-spaces
            n-id, a noun-id structure representing the current noun
    local variables: def-value holds the value of the definite feature
                     from feat-lst
    def-value ← GET-DEF-VALUE(feat-lst)
    case def-value of
        definite :
            for each cur-sid in space-ids do
                when ADD-KNOWN-DEF-ELT(feat-lst n-id cur-sid )
                    return
            add n-id to ment-spaces[FIRST (space-ids)].elements
            return
        indefinite :
            ADD-INDEF-ELT(feat-lst n-id (FIRST (space-ids)))
            return
        zero :
            ADD-ZERO-ELT(feat-lst n-id (FIRST (space-ids)))
            return
```

Figure A.8: ADD-USING-DETERMINERS.

ADD-KNOWN-DEF-ELT tries to find a matching object or bunch among known elements of a *mental-space*. If it succeeds, an appropriate tag is added.

```
function ADD-KNOWN-DEF-ELT (feat-lst n-id space-id)
    returns true if an instance of coreference is identified; false otherwise
    inputs: feat-lst, the current LF
            n-id, a noun-id structure representing the current noun
            space-id, an index in ment-spaces
    local variables: known-elts, a list of elements of the space space-id
    known-elts ← GET-ELEMENTS(ment-spaces[space-id])
    for each el in known-elts do
        when MATCH-NAME (feat-lst el)
            and MATCH-OBJ-BUNCH (feat-lst el)
                no-new-space ← true
                if IS-OBJECT(feat-lst)
                    add n-id to el marked as "object-co-ref"
                else
                    add n-id to el marked as "refers-to-all"
                return true
    return false
```

Figure A.9: ADD-KNOWN-DEF-ELT.

ADD-INDEF-ELT checks to see whether the *mental-space* contains a bunch with the same name as the current noun and inserts the tag *possible-one-of-ref*, if necessary.

```
function ADD-INDEF-ELT(feat-lst n-id space-id)
    inputs: feat-lst, the current LF
            n-id, a noun-id structure representing the current noun
            space-id, an index in ment-spaces
  local variables: known-elts, a list of elements of the space space-id
  known-elts ← GET-ELEMENTS(ment-spaces[space-id])
  for each el in known-elts do
      when IS-BUNCH (el) and MATCH-NAME(feat-lst el)
            add n-id to el marked as "possible-one-of-ref"
  add n-id to ment-spaces[space-id].elements
```

Figure A.10: ADD-INDEF-ELT.

ADD-ZERO-ELT is like ADD-INDEF-ELT, except that the tag here is *possible-part-of-ref*.

```
function ADD-ZERO-ELT(feat-lst n-id space-id)
    inputs: feat-lst, the current LF
            n-id, a noun-id structure representing the current noun
            space-id, an index in ment-spaces
  local variables: known-elts, a list of elements of the space space-id
  known-elts ← GET-ELEMENTS(ment-spaces[space-id])
  for each el in known-elts do
      when IS-BUNCH (el) and MATCH-NAME(feat-lst el)
            add n-id to el marked as "possible-part-of-ref"
  add n-id to ment-spaces[space-id].elements
```

Figure A.11: ADD-ZERO-ELT.

• APPENDIX B •

Implementation of the Heuristic for Ordering Known Spaces

FIND-CLOSEST takes in two arguments, a noun *n* and a list of nouns *W*. It returns a normalized list of values for each element *w* in *W*:

> *(find-closest "door" '("house" "face" "war" "sea")) →*
> *("house" 0.5167507 0.29620022 0.057632707 0.12941638)*

> *(find-closest "eye" '("house" "face" "war" "sea")) →*
> *("face" 0.20473619 0.56622374 0.03303618 0.1960039)*

We could have used existing tools for achieving similar functionality (e.g. the Latent Semantic Analysis (LSA) kit, available at http://lsa.colorado.edu), yet we decided to implement FIND-CLOSEST ourselves. For statistical analysis we were using the Brown corpus (1.5 million words).

In the general case, mutual information is defined as

$$I(X,Y) = \sum_{x,y} p(x,y) \times log_2 \frac{p(x,y)}{f(x)g(y)}$$

where $p(x,y) = P(X{=}x, Y{=}y)$, $f(x) = P(X{=}x)$, $g(y) = P(Y{=}y)$. For our purposes, if *n* and *w* are two words, that have prior probabilities *P(n)* and *P(w)*, their mutual information, according to Fano (1961), can be estimated as

$$I(n,w) = log_2 \frac{P(n,w)}{P(n)P(w)}$$

where *P(n)* and *P(w)* are the numbers of occurrences in the corpus, divided by the size of the corpus, *N*, and *P(n,w)* is the number of co-occurrences of *n* and *w* within a window of a certain size, also divided by *N*. The intuition behind this formula is that if there is a genuine association between *n* and *w*, the value of *P(n,w)* will be higher than the product *P(n)P(w)*, the latter being the probability of co-occurrence in case of conditional independence. Since *P(n)* in the denominator will be the same for all words in *W*, FIND-CLOSEST can simply compare conditional probabilities *P(n,w)/P(w)*. This works reasonably well:

Table B.1: Results for a heuristic computing mutual information

Wind Size	First Arg	house	face	war	sea	OK
200	door	0.36338654	0.41048554	0.090710886	0.135417	
200	window	0.35083807	0.35272947	0.117827915	0.17860456	
200	battle	0.20706688	0.10130909	0.5609199	0.13070413	+
200	soldier	0.12678345	0.18622643	0.53403366	0.15295649	+
200	eye	0.25524414	0.24730016	0.16941336	0.3280423	
200	nose	0.30309263	0.42630225	0.13151872	0.13908644	+
200	ship	0.120281875	0.06899288	0.081802525	0.7289227	+
200	water	0.23830004	0.16937917	0.1325578	0.45976293	+
100	door	0.37568894	0.41646838	0.09019771	0.11764492	
100	window	0.3859844	0.34862682	0.09309612	0.17229266	+
100	battle	0.20854215	0.08617911	0.59959584	0.10568285	+
100	soldier	0.11964532	0.1900461	0.5459638	0.14434478	+
100	eye	0.25904208	0.24472792	0.17962632	0.31660366	
100	nose	0.3104603	0.46541232	0.115322	0.10880543	+
100	ship	0.08656618	0.04125084	0.06279766	0.8093853	+
100	water	0.21540268	0.16793515	0.10751798	0.5091442	+
50	door	0.44948143	0.4226326	0.05059662	0.07728933	+
50	window	0.41173628	0.36512706	0.088281475	0.13485518	+
50	battle	0.16492985	0.06986043	0.62813616	0.13707359	+
50	soldier	0.09461504	0.26049867	0.5662515	0.07863478	+
50	eye	0.27418208	0.26872152	0.19043596	0.26666033	
50	nose	0.26852787	0.4921534	0.12487053	0.11444827	+
50	ship	0.055292573	0.03293528	0.050138585	0.8616336	+
50	water	0.20575051	0.16014016	0.078360185	0.5557491	+

Continued on next page

Table B.1 (continued): Results for a heuristic computing mutual information

Wind Size	First Arg	house	face	war	sea	OK
20	door	0.5143169	0.36817095	0.014924029	0.10258800	+
20	window	0.401384	0.37722495	0.054595463	0.1667956	+
20	battle	0.116694555	0.05148863	0.67017496	0.16164187	+
20	soldier	0.10218534	0.18936452	0.6022922	0.10615809	+
20	eye	0.24941295	0.3053815	0.056541104	0.38866442	
20	nose	0.2514398	0.6656502	0.08290995	0.0	+
20	ship	0.020385832	0.01079370	0.036971215	0.9318493	+
20	water	0.15592422	0.12258511	0.034276374	0.6872143	+
6	door	0.6996893	0.2685872	0.03172346	0.0	+
6	window	0.31521592	0.4228073	0.0	0.2619767	
6	battle	0.15710182	0.05545388	0.5698315	0.21761282	+
6	soldier	0.0	0.59345365	0.40654635	0.0	
6	eye	0.45251572	0.3833502	0.16413414	0.0	
6	nose	0.20116551	0.79883444	0.0	0.0	+
6	ship	0.0	0.0	0.0	1.0	+
6	water	0.12819466	0.0775718	0.033212926	0.7610206	+
4	door	0.7246242	0.27537572	0.0	0.0	+
4	window	0.39059523	0.42672005	0.0	0.18268465	
4	battle	0.22804354	0.05905421	0.39187327	0.32102898	+
4	soldier	0.0	1.0	0.0	0.0	
4	eye	0.57615584	0.4238442	0.0	0.0	
4	nose	0.0	1.0	0.0	0.0	+
4	ship	0.0	0.0	0.0	1.0	+
4	water	0.032312904	0.05122635	0.0	0.9164608	+

Our tests included many more examples (and several variants of the algorithm) but the table above demonstrates general tendencies. Our final implementation of FIND-CLOSEST uses a two-level algorithm based on the presented approach. The performance of the function is sufficient for use in our system. Here are the results for the previous tests and some other examples:

Table B.2: Results for FIND-CLOSEST

First Arg	house	face	war	sea	OK
door	0.5167507	0.29620022	0.057632707	0.12941638	+
window	0.4505913	0.3572705	0.050590888	0.14154732	+
battle	0.23767237	0.21234927	0.4300339	0.11994449	+
soldier	0.22959097	0.23347236	0.38978612	0.1471505	+
eye	0.20473619	0.56622374	0.03303618	0.1960039	+
nose	0.21825175	0.5736857	0.056811374	0.15125115	+
ship	0.17755279	0.17756595	0.11521427	0.529667	+
water	0.20192678	0.20709926	0.08495047	0.50602347	+

Table B.3: Results for FIND-CLOSEST (additional set)

First Art	bird	sea	ship	music	OK
seagull	0.51303184	0.10357396	0.3833942	0.0	+
parrot	0.42860296	0.2064908	0.32202348	0.04288271	+
cruise	0.24961056	0.18011189	0.5151701	0.05510755	+
sail	0.19635014	0.22922061	0.5295479	0.04488133	+
concert	0.25334337	0.07754358	0.15204084	0.51707226	+
piano	0.23765689	0.08881465	0.1390381	0.53449035	+
water	0.24937329	0.50918317	0.19689792	0.04454564	+
wave	0.20423165	0.41523913	0.36666125	0.01386795	+

Each noun to be processed by FIND-CLOSEST—the first argument *n* and all words in *W*—is represented by a structure *wstruct* with fields:

name, the word itself
closest-in-corpus, a list
cooccur-counts, a map from words to integers
result, a number

Initially *closest-in-corpus* consists of only the noun itself and its plural (if it exists), *cooccur-counts* is empty. The function COUNT-IN-CORPUS for each word in *closest-in-corpus* collects as keys in *cooccur-counts* all words that co-occur with *name* in the corpus within a window of size 10. The values in *cooccur-counts* show how many times each key co-occurs with *name*. A significant improvement in the performance has been achieved by ignoring words that occur in the corpus fewer than 10 times.

After the first call to COUNT-IN-CORPUS we put in *closest-in-corpus* 30 words with highest scores in *cooccur-counts* (for each word, its count is first divided by the square root of the number of its total occurrences in the corpus). After that *cooccur-counts* is cleared. Then COUNT-IN-CORPUS is called again with *wstruct*s of every word in *W*, the difference being that they have 30 words in *closest-in-corpus* now, instead of 2. After the second iteration of the algorithm each *cooccur-counts* map will contain approximately 5 to 10 thousand entries.

Finally, the *result* field of the *wstruct* of each word in *W* is set to the sum of the values in its *cooccur-counts* of each word *l* from the *closest-in-corpus* list of *n* (divided by the square root of the number of occurrences of *l* in the corpus). Note that the *closest-in-corpus* list of *n* at this point contains 30 words because its *wstruct* was updated during the first iteration together with the elements of *W*.

```
function FIND-CLOSEST(n, W)
    inputs: n, a noun
            W, a list of nouns
    local variables: wst-n, a wstruct corresponding to n
                     wst-W, a list of wstructs corresponding
                            to the elements of W
    for each wst in wst-W and wst-n do
            wst.closest-in-corpus ← [wst.name | GET-PLURAL(wst.name)]
            COUNT-IN-CORPUS(wst)
            wsi.closest-in-corpus ← SELECT-TOP-N(wst.cooccur-counts, 30)
            CLEAR(wst.cooccur-counts)
    for each wst in wst-W do
            COUNT-IN-CORPUS(wst)
            for each l in wst-n.closest-in-corpus do
                wst.result ← wst.result +
                            wst.cooccur-counts[l]/SQRT (OCCUR-NUM(l))
    return GET-RESULTS(wst-W)
```

Figure B.1: The FIND-CLOSEST algorithm.

Bibliography

Abbott, B. 2004. Definiteness and indefiniteness. The handbook of pragmatics, ed. by L. R. Horn and G. Ward, 122–149. Oxford: Blackwell.

Abney, Steven. 1987. The English noun phrase in its sentential aspect. Cambridge, MA: Dissertation.

Abraham, Werner. 1996. Kasus, Aspekt und norninale Referenz: Komplexe kausale Zusammenhänge in der Diachronie des Deutschen und ihre formale Darstellung auf vergleichender typologischer Grundlage. Language Change and Generative Grammar, ed. by Ellen Brandner, Gisella Ferraresi, 22–70. Opladen: Westdeutscher Verlag.

———. 1997. The interdependence of case, aspect and referentiality in the history of German: the case of the verbal genitive. Parameters of morphosyntactic change, ed. by Ans van Kemenade and Nigel Vincent, 29–61. Cambridge, UK: Cambridge University Press.

Allen, James F., Bradford W. Miller, Eric K. Ringger, Teresa Sikorski. 1996. A robust system for natural spoken dialogue. Proceedings of the 34th Annual Meeting of the Association for Computational Linguistics (ACL '96). 62 70.

Alshawi, H. 1987. Memory and context for language interpretation. Cambridge, UK: Cambridge University Press.

Appelt, Douglas. 1985. Planning English referring expressions. Artificial Intelligence 26 (1). 1–33.

Appelt, Douglas, and Amichai Kronfeld. 1987. A computational model of referring. Proceedings of the International Joint Conference on Articial Intelligence (IJCAI) 1987, vol. 2. Milan. 640–647.

Ariel, M. 1988. Referring and accessibility. Journal of Linguistics 24. 67–87.

———. 1990. Accessing noun-phrase antecedents. London: Routlege.

———. 2001. Accessibility theory: An overview. Text representation, ed. by T. Sanders, J. Schliperoord, and W. Spooren, 29–87. Amsterdam/Philadelphia: John Benjamins.

Arnold, E. 1952. Zur Geschichte der Suppositionstheorie. Symposion. Jahrbuch für Philosophie. Freiburg, München: Karl Alber. 3–134.

Ash, R.B. 1965. Information theory. New York, NY: Interscience Publishers.

Azzam S., K. Humphreys, and R. Gaizauskas. 1998. Evaluating a focus-based approach to anaphora resolution. Proceedings COLING-ACL '98, Montreal, Canada. vol. I. 74–78.

Bacon, John. 1973 a. Do generic descriptions denote? Mind 327. 331–347.

———. 1973 b. The semantics of generic the. Journal of Philosophical Logic 2. 323–339.

Barth E.M. 1974. The logic of the articles in traditional philosophy. Dordrecht, Boston: D. Reidel.

Bartsch, Karl. 1870. Der Nibelunge Nôt. Leipzig: Brockhaus.

Barwise, Jon, and Robin Cooper. 1981. Generalized quantifiers and natural language. Linguistics and Philosophy 4(2). 159–220.

Barwise, Jon, and John Perry. 1983. Situations and attitudes. Cambridge, MA: MIT Press.

Bechstein, Reinhold (ed.). 1873. Gottfried's von Strassburg Tristan. Leipzig: F. A. Brockhaus.

Behaghel, Otto. 1923–1932. Deutsche Syntax. 4 vol. Heidelberg: Carl Winter.

Bell, Robert Mowry. 1907. Der Artikel bei Otfrid. Leipzig: Dissertation.

Benn, Gottfried. 1990. Gehirne. Deutschland erzählt. Von Arthur Schnitzler bis Uwe Johnson, ed. by Benno von Wiese, 83–87. Frankfurt am Main: Fischer.

Bierwisch, Manfred. 1983. Semantische und konzeptuelle Repräsentationen lexikalischer Einheiten. Untersuchungen zur Semantik, ed. by Rudolf Ruzicka and Wolfgang Motsch, 61–100. Berlin: Akademie.

Birkenmaier, Willy. 1977. Aspekt, Aktionsart und nominale Determination im Russischen. Zeitschrift für Slavische Philologie 39. 398–417.

Birner, Betsy, Gregory Ward. 1994. Uniqueness, familiarity, and the definite article in English. Proceedings of the Annual Meeting of the Berkeley Linguistic Society. 93–102.

Birner, B. J., G. Ward. 1998. Information status and noncanonical word order in English. Amsterdam, Philadelphia: John Benjamins.

Bisle-Müller. Hansjörg. 1991. Artikelwörter im Deutschen. Tübingen: Niemeyer.

Bittner, Dagmar. 1997. Entfaltung gramnmatischer Relationen im NP-Erwerb: Referenz. Folia Linguistica 31. 255–283.

Bouchard, Denis. 1985. The binding theory and the notion of accessible SUBJECT. Linguistic Inquiry 16. 117–133.

Bouma, Gosse 1988: Modifiers and specifiers in categorial unification grammar. Linguistics 26. 21–46.

Braune, Wilhelm. 1987. Althochdeutsche Grammatik, bearbeitet von Hans Eggers. Tübingen: Niemeyer.

Braunmüller, Kurt. 1977. Referenz und Pronominalisierung. Zu den Deiktika und Proformen des Deutschen. Tübingen: Niemeyer.

Brown, P., S. Della Pietra, V. Della Pietra, R. Mercer. 1991. Word sense disambiguation using statistical methods. Proceedings of the 29th Meeting of the Association for Computational Linguistics (ACL-91). Berkley, CA. 264–270.

Brunhuber, Brigitte. 1983. Aspekt und Determiniertheit im Russischen. Die slawischen Sprachen 3. 5–13.

Burton-Roberts, Noel. 1976. On the generic indefinite article. Language 52 (2). 427–448.

———. 1977. Generic sentences and analyticity. Studies in Language 1. 155–196.

Butcher, S.H. 1898. Aristotle's Theory of Poetry and Fine Art. London: Macmillan.

Bybee, Joan L. 1985. Morphology. A study of the relation between meaning and form. Amsterdam: Benjamins.

Byron, Donna K., and James F. Allen. 2002. What's a reference resolution module to do? Proceedings of the 4th Discourse Anaphora and Anaphora Resolution Colloquium (DAARC2002). 80–87.

Carlson, G. N. 1977. A unified analysis of the English bare plural. Linguistics and Philosophy 1. 413–456.

———. 1980. Reference to kinds in English. New York, London: Garland.

———. 1982. Generic terms and generic sentences. Journal of philosophical logic 11. 145–181.

Carnap, Rudolf. 1947. Meaning and necessity. A study in semantics and modal logic. Chicago: The University of Chicago Press.

Chafe, Wallace L. 1994. Discourse, consciousness, and time: the flow and displacement of conscious experience in speaking and writing. Chicago: Chicago University Press.

Chatman, Seymour 1960. Pre-adjectivals in the English Nominal Phrase. American Speech 35. 83–99.

Christophersen, Paul. 1939. The articles. A study of their theory and use in English. Kopenhagen, London: Munksgaard.

Chur, Jeannette. 1993. Generische Nominalphrasen im Deutschen. Tübingen: Niemeyer.

Church, K., and P. Hanks. 1990. Word association norms, mutual information, and lexicography. Computational Linguistics 16. 22–29.

Clark, H. H., S. E. Haviland. 1977. Comprehension and the given-new contrast. Discourse processes: Advances in research and theory. Vol. 1: Discourse Production and Comprehension, ed. by R. Freedle, 1–40. Norwood, NJ: Ablex.

Cochiarelia, Nino. 1979. The theory of homogenous simple types as a second order logic. Notre Dame Journal of Formal Logic 20. 552–564.

Dale R. 1992. Generating referring expressions: building descriptions in a domain of objects and processes. Cambridge, MA: MIT Press.

Delbrück, Berthold. 1910. Beiträge zur germanischen Syntax I. Der altisländische Artikel. Beiträge zur Geschichte der deutschen Sprache und Literatur 36. 355–359.

Devitt M., and K. Sterelny. 1999. Language and reality: an introduction to the philosophy of language. Cambridge, MA: MIT Press.

Diebich, Rainer. 1985. Zum Begriff der Determination. Foreign Languages 3. 7–18.

Diesing, Molly. 1992. Indefinites. Cambridge, MA: MIT Press.

Diewald, Gabriele Maria. 1991. Deixis und Textsorten im Deutschen. Tübingen: Niemeyer.

Dinneen, Francis P. 1967. An introduction to general linguistics. New York: Holt, Rinehart and Winston.

Donnellan, K. S. 1966. Reference and definite descriptions. Philosophical Review 75. 281 304.

Doron, Edit. 1988. The semantics of predicate nominals. Linguistics 26. 281–301.

DPTAC. 2003. Making private hire services more accessible to disabled people. http://www.dptac.gov.uk/pubs/phv/03.htm

Du Bois, J. W. 1980. Beyond definiteness: The trace of identity in discourse. The pear stories: Cognitive, cultural, and linguistic aspects of narrative production, ed. by Wallace L. Chafe, 203–274. Norwood, NJ: Ablex.

DUDEN. 1998. Grammatik der deutschen Gegenwartssprache. Hg. von der Dudenredaktion. Bearb. von Peter Eisenberg. Mannheim u. a. Vol. 4. Mannheim: Dudenverlag.

Dreiser, Theodore. 1946. The financier. Cleveland: World.

Eroms, Hans-Werner. 1988. Der Artikel im Deutschen und seine dependenzgrammatische Darstellung. Sprachwissenschaft 13. 257–308.

Fano, R. 1961. Transmission of information. Cambridge, MA: MIT Press.

Fauconnier, Gilles. 1985. Mental Spaces. Cambridge, MA: MIT Press.

Fauconnier, Gilles, and Eve Sweetser. 1996. Spaces, Worlds, and Grammar. Chicago: University of Chicago Press.

Fillmore, Charles. 1976. Frame semantics and the nature of language. Annals of the New York Academy of Sciences 280. 20–32.

———. 1988. The mechanisms of construction grammar. Berkeley Linguistics Society 14. 35–55.

Flämig, Walter. 1991. Grammatik des Deutschen. Berlin: Akademie.

Fleischer W. 1967. Zur Funktion des Artikels in der deutschen Sprache der Gegenwart. Acta Universitatis Wratislaviensis 60. Wrocław. 131–160.

Flom, George T. 1910. The scope of the post-positive article in Olafs Saga hins Helga. The Journal of English and Germanic Philology 9. 193–223.

Fodor, Janet D., and Ivan Sag. 1982. Referential and quantificational indefinites. Linguistics and Philosophy 5. 355–398.

Fraurud, K. 1990. Definiteness and the processing of NPs in natural discourse. Journal of Semantics 7. 395–433.

———. 1992. Processing Noun Phrases in natural discourse. Stockholm University: Dissertation.

Frege, Gottlob. 1892. Über Begriff und Gegenstand. Vierteljahresschrift für wissenschaftliche Philosophie 16. 192–205.

Gadamer, Hans-Georg, and Gottfried Boehm (ed.). 1976. Seminar: Philosophische Hermeneutik. Frankfurt am Main: Suhrkampf.

Gaizauskas R., and K. Humphreys. 1997. Using a semantic network for information extraction. Natural Language Engineering 3 (2–3). 147–169.

Gil, David. 1987. Definiteness, Noun Phrase configurationality, and the count-mass distinction. The representation of (in)definiteness, ed. by Eric Reuland and Alice ter Meulen, 254–269. Cambridge, MA: MIT Press.

Givón, Talmy. 1981. On the development of the numeral *one* as an indefinite marker. Folia Linguistica Historica 2. 35–53.

Gladrow, Wolfgang. 1972. Sprachliche Mittel zum Ausdruck der Determiniertheit/ Indeterminiertheit. Zeitschrift für Slawistik 17. 647–656.

———. 1979. Die Determination des Substantivs im Russischen und Deutschen: eine konfrontative Studie. Leipzig: Enzyklopädie.

Goffman E. 1969. Verhalten in sozialen Situationen: Strukturen und Regeln der Interaktion im öffentlichen Raum. Gütersloh: Bertelsmann.

———. 1974. Frame analysis. Cambridge, MA: Harvard University Press.

Graf, Heinrich. 1905. Die Entwicklung des deutschen Artikels vom Althochdeutschen zum Mittelhochdeutschen. Giessen: Dissertation.

Grasserie, Raoul de la. 1896. De l'article (Morphologie et syntaxe). Mémoires de la Société de Linguistique de Paris 9. 285–322, 381–394.

Grice, H.P. 1975. Logic and conversation. Speech Acts, ed. by P. Cole and J. Morgan, 41–58. New York: Academic Press.

Grimm, H.-J. 1981a. Zu einigen deutschen Genitivkonstruktionen mit Nullartikel. Deutsch als Fremdsprache 18. 278 –280.

———. 1981b. Zum Artikelgebrauch in deutschen Funktionsverbgefügen mit Präpositionen. Deutsch als Fremdsprache 18. 333–337.

———. 1981c. Einige Beobachtungen zum Artikelgebrauch in Zeitungsüberschriften. Sprachpflege 30, 129.

———. 1982. Zur Unterscheidung von *ein* als unbestimmtem Artikel und als Numerale. Wissenschaftliche Zeitschrift der Humboldt-Universität zu Berlin. Geselschafts- und sprachwissenschaftliche Reihe 31. Berlin. 329–341.

———. 1987. Lexikon zum Artikelgebrauch. Leipzig: Enzyklopädie.

Grosz, Barbara. 1977. The representation and use of focus in dialogue understanding. Berkeley, CA: University of California at Berkeley: Dissertation.

Grosz, Barbara 1978. Focusing in dialogue. Theoretical Issues in Natural Language Processing 2. Urbana, Illinois. 96–103.

———. 1981. Focusing and descriptions in natural language. Elements of Discourse Understanding, ed. by A. Joshi, 84–105. Cambridge, UK: Cambridge University Press.

Grosz, Barbara, and C.L, Sidner. 1986. Attentions, intentions and the structure of discourse. Computational Linguistics 12 (3). 175–204.

Grosz, Barbara, A.K. Joshi, and S. Weinstein. 1995. Centering: A framework for modeling the local coherence of discourse. Computational Linguistics 21(2). 203–225.

Guillaume, G. 1919. Le problème de l'article et sa solution dans la langue française. Paris: Hachette et Cie.

Gundel, Jeanette K., N. Hedberg, and R. Zacharski. 1988. The generation and interpretation of demonstrative expressions. Proceedings of the XIIth International Conference on Computational Linguistics. John Von Neumann Society for the Computing Sciences, Budapest. 216-221.

Gundel, Jeanette K., N. Hedberg, and R. Zacharski. 1989. Givenness, implicature, and demonstrative expressions in English discourse. Chicago Linguistic Society. 25(2). 89–103.

Gundel, Jeanette K., N. Hedberg, and R. Zacharski. 1993. Cognitive status and the form of referring expressions in discourse. Language, 69(2). 274–307.

Gundel, Jeanette K., and A. Mulkern. 1998. Quantity implicatures in reference understanding. Pragmatics and Cognition: Special Issue on the Concept of Reference in the Cognitive Sciences 6. 21–45.

Habermas J. 1995. Theorie des kommunikativen Handelns. Bd. 2: Zur Kritik der funktionalistischen Vernunft. Frankfurt am Main: Suhrkamp.

Hartmann, Dietrich. 1967. Studien zum bestimmten Artikel in Morant und Galie und anderen rheinischen Denkmälern des Mittelalters. Giessen: Schmitz.

Harweg R. 1969. Unbestimmter und bestimmter Artikel in generalisierender Funktion. Orbis: Bulletin international de Documentation linguistique, Louvain, 18(2). 297–331.

Haspelmath, M. 1997. Indefinite pronouns. Oxford: Oxford University Press.

Hawkins, John A. 1977. The pragmatics of definiteness. Linguistische Berichte 47. 1–27

———. 1978. Definiteness and indefiniteness: a study in reference and grammaticality prediction. London: Croom Helm.

———. 1991. On (in)definite articles: implicatures and (un)grammaticality prediction. Journal of Linguistics 27. 405–442.

Hayes P.J. 1980. The logic of frames. Frame conceptions and text understanding, ed. by D. Metzing, 46–61. Berlin, New York: Walter de Gruyter.

Heeman, P. A., and J. F. Allen. 1995. The TRAINS-93 dialogues. TRAINS technical note TN 94-2, University of Rochester Department of Computer Science, Rochester, NY.

Heim, Irene. 1982. The semantics of definite and indefinite noun phrases. Konstanz: Universität.

———. 1983. File change semantics and the familiarity theory of definiteness. Meaning, use and the interpretation of language, ed. by R. Bäuerle, C. Schwarze, and A. von Stechow, 164–189. Berlin: Walter de Gruyter.

Heinrichs, H.M. 1954. Studien zum bestimmten Artikel in den germanischen Sprachen. Giessen: Wilhelm Schmitz Verlag.

Helbig, Gerhard, and Joachim Buscha. 1975. Deutsche Grammatik. Ein Handbuch für den Ausländerunterricht. Leipzig: Enzyklopädie.

Hermanns, Fritz. 1980. Es gibt eigennamen von handlungen. Beantwortung einer preisfrage. Zeitschrift für Germanistische Linguistik 8. 93–95.

Heyer, Gerhard. 1985. Generic descriptions, default reasoning, and typicality. Theoretical Linguistics 12. 33–72.

———. 1987. Generische Kennzeichnungen. Zur Logik und Ontologie generischer Bedeutung. München, Wien: Philosophia.

Himmelmann, Nikolaus P. 1997. Deiktikon, Artikel, Nominalphrase. Zur Emergenz syntaktischer Struktur. Tübingen: Niemeyer.

———. 1998. Regularity in irregularity: article use in adpositional phrases. Linguistic Typology 2. 315–353.

Hodler, Werner. 1954. Grundzüge einer germanischen Artikellehre. Heidelberg: Carl Winter.

Hu, Kung-Zeng. 1980. Der Gebrauch des Artikels in der deutschen Gegenwartssprache. Freiburg, Schweiz: Universitätsverlag.

Husserl, Edmund. 1980. Logische Untersuchungen. Tübingen: Niemeyer.

———. 1985. Erfahrung und Urteil. Hamburg: Meiner.

Jackendoff, Ray S. 1977. X' Syntax: A study of phrase structure. (Linguistic Inquiry monograph 2). Cambridge, MA: MIT Press.

Jackendoff, Ray S. 1983. Semantics and Cognition. Cambridge, MA: MIT Press.

Jäger, Paul. 1917. Der Gebrauch des bestimmten Artikels bei Isidor und Tatian vergleichend dargestellt. Leipzig. Dissertation.

Janson, Tore. 1984. Articles and plural formation in creoles: Change and Universals. Lingua 64. 291–323.

Johnsen, Gail Perkins. 1976. The development of the definite article in Old Norse. The University of Rochester: Dissertation.

Jurafsky, Daniel, and James H. Martin. 2000. Speech and language processing. Upper Saddle River, N.J.: Prentice Hall.

Kafka, Franz. 1971. The complete stories. Edited by Nahum N. Glatzer. New York: Schocken Books.

———. 1990. Der Jäger Gracchus. Deutschland erzählt. Von Arthur Schnitzler bis Uwe Johnson, ed. by Benno von Wiese, 63–67. Frankfurt am Main: Fischer.

Kamp, H. , and U. Reyle. 1993. From discourse to logic: introduction to model-theoretic semantics of natural language, formal logic and discourse representation theory. Dordrecht: Kluwer.

Karttunen, Lauri. 1976. Discourse referents. Notes from the linguistic underground, ed. by J.D. McCawley, 363–385. New York, NY: Academic Press.

Kästner, Erich. 1950. Kurz und bündig. Epigramme. Zürich: Atrium.

Keenan, Edward L., and Jonathan Stavi. 1986. A semantic characterization of natural language determiners. Linguistics and Philosophy 9. 253–327.

Kennedy C., and B. Boguraev. 1996. Anaphora in a wider context: tracking discourse referents. Proceedings ECAI '96. Budapest, Hungary. 582–586.

Kolde, Gottfried. 1988. Indefinitheit und Nichtfaktizität. Anmerkungen zur Semantik des unbestimmten Artikels im Deutschen. Linguistik Parisette. Akten des 22. Linguistischen Kolloquiums Paris 1987. Tübingen: Niemeyer. 29–40.

———. 1989. Der Artikel in deutschen Sachverhaltsnominalen. Tübingen: Niemeyer.

———. 1996. Nominaldetermination. Eine systematische und kommentierte Bibliographie unter besonderer Berücksichtigung des Deutschen, Englischen und Französischen. Tübingen: Niemeyer.

Kovari, Geoffrey. 1984. Studien zum germanischen Artikel. Entstehung und Verwendung des Artikels im Gotischen. Wien: Peter Lang.

Krámský, J. 1972. The article and the concept of definiteness in language. The Hague, Paris: Mouton.
Krippendorff K. 1980. Content analysis: an introduction to its methodology. Beverly Hills, CA: Sage Publications.
Kronfeld, A. 1986. Donnellan's distinction and a computational model of reference. Proceedings 24th Annual Meeting of the ACL, New York, NY. 186–191.
Kurrelmeyer, Wilhelm (ed.). 1904. Die erste deutsche Bibel. (Druck Strassburg, Johann Mentel(in). 1466). Vol. 1. Evangelien. Tübingen: Literarischer Verein in Stuttgart.
Lambrecht, Knud. 1994. Information structure and sentence form: topic, focus, and the mental representations of discourse referents. Cambridge, UK: Cambridge University Press.
Langacker, Ronald W. 2001. Discourse in cognitive grammar. Cognitive Linguistics 12(2). 143–188.
Lappin, Shalom, and Herbert Leass. 1994. An algorithm for pronominal anaphora resolution. Computational Linguistics 20(4). 535–561.
Lehnert W.G. 1980. The role of scripts in understanding. Frame conceptions and text understanding, ed. by D. Metzing, 79–95. Berlin, New York: Walter de Gruyter.
Leiss, Elisabeth. 1994. Die Entstehung des Artikels im Deutschen. Sprachwissenschaft 19. 307–319.
———. 1997. Genus im Althochdeutschen. Grammatica ianua artium: Festschrift für Rolf Bergmann zum 60. Geburtstag, ed. by Elvira Glaser and Michael Schlaefer, 33–48. Heidelberg: Carl Winter.
———. 2000. Artikel und Aspekt: die grammatischen Muster von Definitheit. Berlin: Walter De Gruyter.
Lewis, D. 1979. Scorekeeping in a language game. Journal of Philosophical Logic 8. 339–359.
Link, Godehard. 1983. The logical alysis of plurals and mass terms: a lattice-theoretical approach. Meaning, use and interpretation of language, ed. by Rainer Bäuerle, Christoph Schwarze, Arnim von Stechow, 302–323. Berlin, New York: Walter De Gruyter.
Löbner, Sebastian. 1985. Definites. Journal of Semantics 4. 279–326.
———. 1986. In Sachen Nullartikel. Linguistische Berichte 101. 64–66.
———. 1990. Wahr neben Falsch. Duale Operatoren als die Quantoren natürlicher Sprache. Tübingen: Niemeyer.
Lumsden, M. 1988. Existential sentences: Their structure and meaning. London: Croom Helm.
Lyons, Christopher. 1999. Definiteness. Cambridge, UK: Cambridge University Press.
Mann, Thomas. 1955. Doktor Faustus. Gesammelte Werke. Bd. 6. Berlin: Aufbau.
Maratsos, Michael P. 1976. The use of definite and indefinite reference in young children. An experimental study of semantic acquisition. Cambridge, UK: Cambridge University Press.
Matsui, T. 2000. Bridging and relevance. Amsterdam: John Benjamins.
Mayer, Anna. 1916. Die historische Entwicklung des Artikels in prapositionaler Verbindung im Frlihneuhochdeutschen. Heidelberg: Dissertation.
Mayer, Rolf. 1981. Ontologische Aspekte der Nominalsemantik. Tübingen: Niemeyer.
Metzing, D. (ed.). 1980. Frame conceptions and text understanding. Berlin, New York: Walter de Gruyter.
Milsark, G. 1977. Toward an explanation of certain peculiarities of the existential construction in English. Linguistic analysis 3. 1–29.
Minsky, M. A framework for representing knowledge. Frame conceptions and text understanding, ed. by D. Metzing, 1–25. Berlin, New York: Walter de Gruyter.

Mollay, Karl (ed.). 1971. Die Denkwürdigkeiten der Helene Kottannerin (1439–1440). Wien: Österreichischer Bundesverlag.

Montague, Richard. 1974. The proper treatment of quantification in ordinary English. Formal philosophy. Selected papers of Richard Montague, ed. by Richmond Thomason, 247–270. New Haven, London: Yale University Press.

Neale, S. 1990. Descriptions. Cambridge, MA: MIT Press.

Neumann, Reinulf. 1967. Der bestimmte Artikel ther und thie und seine Funktionen im althochdeutschen Tatian. Beiträge zur deutschen Philologie 37. Giessen: W. Schmitz.

Norvig, Peter. 1992. Paradigms of artificial intelligence programming. San Mateo, CA: Morgan Kaufmann.

Notker der Deutsche. 1983. Die Werke Notkers des Deutschen. Vol. 10. Der Psalter. Psalm 101–150, ed. By Petrus W. Tax. Tübingen: Niemeyer.

Ockham, Wilhelm von. 1984. Texte zur Theorie der Erkenntnis und der Wissenschaft. Lateinisch/Deutsch. Herausgegeben, übersetzt und kommentiert von R. Isbach. Stuttgart: Reclam.

Oomen, Ingelore. 1977. Determination bei generischen, definiten und indefiniten Beschreibungen im Deutschen. Linguistische Arbeiten 53. Tübingen: Niemeyer.

Ostertag, G. (ed.). 1998. Definite descriptions: A reader. Cambridge, MA: MIT Press.

Partee, Barbara. 1987. Noun phrase interpretation and type-shifting principles. Studies in discourse representation theory and the theory of generalized quantifiers, ed. by Jeroen Groenendijk, Dick de Jongh, Martin Stokhof, 115–143. Dordrecht: Foris.

Paul, Hermann. 1959. Mittelhochdeutsche Grammatik. Bearbeitet von Walther Mitzka. Tübingen: Niemeyer.

Philippi, Julia. 1997. The rise of the article in the Germanic languages. Parameters of Morphosyntactic Change, ed. by Ans van Kemenade and Nigel Vincent, 62–93. Cambridge, UK: Cambridge University Press.

Piattelli-Palmarini, M. (ed.). 1980. Language and learning. The debate between Jean Piaget and Noam Chomsky. Cambridge, MA: Harvard University Press.

Platteau, Frank. 1980. Definite and indefinite generics. The semantics of determiners, ed. by Johan Van der Auwera, 112–123. London: Croom Helm.

Poesio, M., and R. Vieira. 1998. A corpus-based investigation of definite description use. Computational Linguistics 24. 183–216.

Popescu-Belis, A. 2003. Evaluation-driven design of a robust reference resolution system. Natural Language Engineering 9 (3). 281–306.

Postal, P. M. 1966. On so-called pronouns in English. The Nineteenth Monograph on Language and Linguistics, ed. by F. Dinneen, 191–224. Washington, D.C.: Georgetown University Press.

Presslich, Marion. 1993. Die Entstehung und Entwicklung des unbestimmten Artikels im Althochdeutschen. Zulassungsarbeit im Studiengang Germanistik, Universität Erlangen-Nürnberg.

Prince, Ellen. 1978. A comparison of wh-clefts and it-clefts in discourse. Language 54. 883–906.

———. 1981a. Toward a taxonomy of given-new information. Radical Pragmatics, ed. by P. Cole, 223–256. New York: Academic Press.

———. 1981b. On the inferencing of indefinite this NPs. Elements of discourse understanding, ed. by A.K. Joshi, B.L. Webber, and I.A. Sag, 231–250. Cambridge, UK: Cambridge University Press.

———. 1992. The ZPG letter: Subjects, definiteness, and information status. Discourse description: diverse analyses of a fund-raising text, ed. by S. Thompson and W. Mann, 295–325. New York: John Benjamins.
Quine, Willard van Orman. 1960. World and object. Cambridge, MA: MIT Press.
Radford, Andrew. 1988. Transformational grammar: a first course. New York: Cambridge University Press.
Rauch, Irmengard. 1983. Modality of Article. Monatshefte 75. 156–162.
Reimer, M., and A. Bezuidenhout (eds.) 2004. Descriptions and beyond. Oxford: Oxford University Press.
Reis, Marga 1977. Präsuppositionen und Syntax. Tübingen: Niemeyer.
Reiter, Norbert. 1977. Die Artikelopposition im Deutschen. Linguistics 190. 35–46.
Reuland, Eric J., and Alice G. ter Meulen (eds.) 1987. The representation of (in)definiteness. Cambridge, MA: MIT Press.
Roberts, C. 2003. Uniqueness in definite noun phrases. Linguistics and Philosophy 26. 287–350.
Rosch, Eleanor. 1973. Natural categories. Cognitive Psychology 4. 328–350.
Russell, Stuart J., and Peter Norvig. 2003. Artificial intelligence: a modern approach. Upper Saddle River, NJ: Prentice Hall/Pearson Education.
Sabatini, Rafael. 1976. Captain Blood. Toronto, New York: Bantam.
Salton G., and M.J. McGill. 1983. Introduction to modern information retrieval. New York, NY: McGraw-Hill.
Schank R., and R. Abelson. 1977. Scripts, plans, goals and understanding. Hillsdale, NJ: Lawrence Erlbaum.
Schlosser, Horst Dieter (ed.). 2004. Althochdeutsche Literatur. Berlin: Erich Schmidt.
Sidner, C.L. 1979. Towards a computational theory of definite anaphora comprehension in English discourse. Cambridge, MA: Dissertation.
Sidner, C.L. 1981. Focusing for interpretation of pronouns. American Journal of Computational Linguistics 7 (4). 217–231.
Sievers, Eduard (ed.). 1892. Tatian: lateinisch und altdeutsch. Paderborn: Schöningh.
Simon J. 1971. Philosophie und linguistische Theorie. Berlin, New York: Walter de Gruyter.
Simons, Peter M. 1996. Mereology and set theory as competing methodological tools within philosophy of language. Sprachphilosophie. Bd. 2, ed. by Marcelo Dascal, Dietfried Gerhardus, Kuno Lorenz, Geord Meggle, 1085–1097. Berlin: de Gruyter.
Spangler, Wayne E. 1975. Rethinking the category determiner. Linguistics 143. 61–74.
Sperber, D, and D. Wilson. 1986. Relevance: communication and cognition. Cambridge, MA: Harvard University Press.
Stalnaker, R. C. 1974. Pragmatic presuppositions. Semantics and philosophy, ed. by M. Munitz and P. Unger, 197–214. New York: New York University.
Strawson, P.F. 1950. On referring. Mind 59. 320–344.
Strigin, Anatoli. 1985. Eine Semantik für generische Sätze. Linguistische Studien, Reihe A 125. 1–85.
Ter Meulen, Alice. 1986. Generic information, conditional contexts and constraints. On conditionals, ed. by Elizabeth Traugott, Charles Ferguson, 123–145. Cambridge, UK: Cambridge Universi Press.
Thrane, Torben. 1980. Referential-semantic analysis. Cambridge, UK: Cambridge University Press.

Turner, Raymond. 1987. Formal semantics and type-free theories. Studies in discourse representation theory and the theory of generalized quantifier, ed. by Jeroen Groenendijk, 145–159. Dordrecht: Foris.

Van Valin, Robert D. 2001. An introduction to syntax. New York: Cambridge University Press.

Vater, Heinz. 1970. Zur Tiefenstruktur deutscher Nominalphrasen. Vorschläge fur eine strukturale Grammatik des Deutschen, ed. by H. Steger, 121–149. Darmstadt: Wissenschaftliche Buchgesellschaft.

———. 1979. Das System der Artikelformen im gegenwärtigen Deutsch. Tübingen: Niemeyer.

———. 1984. Determinantien und Quantoren im Deutschen. Zeitschrift für Sprachwissenschaft 3. 19–42.

——— (ed.). 1986a. Zur Syntax der Determinantien. Tubingen: Niemeyer.

———. 1986b. Einführung in die Referenzsemantik. Köln: Institut für deutsche Sprache und Literatur.

Werner, Otmar. 1978. Der bestimmte Artikel als All-Quantor. Sprache in Gegenwart und Geschichte. Festschrift fur H.M. Heinrichs, ed. by D. Hartmann, 215–235. Köln/Wien: Böhlau.

Witzig, Eva. 1910. Zum Gebrauche des Artikels im Althochdeutschen. Bonn: Dissertation.

BERKELEY INSIGHTS IN LINGUISTICS AND SEMIOTICS

Irmengard Rauch
General Editor

Through the publication of groundbreaking scholarly research, this series deals with language and the multiple and varied paradigms through which it is studied. Language as viewed by linguists represents micrometa-approaches that intersect with macrometa-approaches of semiotists who understand language as an inlay to all experience. This data-based series bridges study of the sciences with that of the humanities.

www.ingramcontent.com/pod-product-compliance
Ingram Content Group UK Ltd.
Pitfield, Milton Keynes, MK11 3LW, UK
UKHW021827100926
8556IPUK00003B/209

9 781433 102240